ANCIENT SOUTH ARABIA

FROM THE QUEEN OF SHEBA TO THE ADVENT OF ISLAM

Ancient South Arabia

FROM THE QUEEN OF SHEBA TO THE ADVENT OF ISLAM

KLAUS SCHIPPMANN

Translated from German by Allison Brown

Markus Wiener Publishers
Princeton

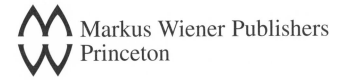

The translation of this book has been supported by a grant
from InterNationes, Bonn.

For information write to: Markus Wiener Publishers
231 Nassau Street, Princeton, NJ 08542

Library of Congress Cataloging-in-Publication Data

Schippmann, Klaus.
[Geschichte der alt-südarabischen Reiche. English]
Ancient South Arabia: From the Queen of Sheba to the Advent of Islam/
by Klaus Schippmann;
translated from the German by Allison Brown.
Includes bibliographical references and index.
ISBN 1-55876-235-3 hardcover
ISBN 1-55876-236-1 paperback
1. Arabia, Southern—History. I. Title.
DS247.A147 S35 2000
939'.49—dc21 99-086421

Printed in the United States of America on acid-free paper.

CONTENTS

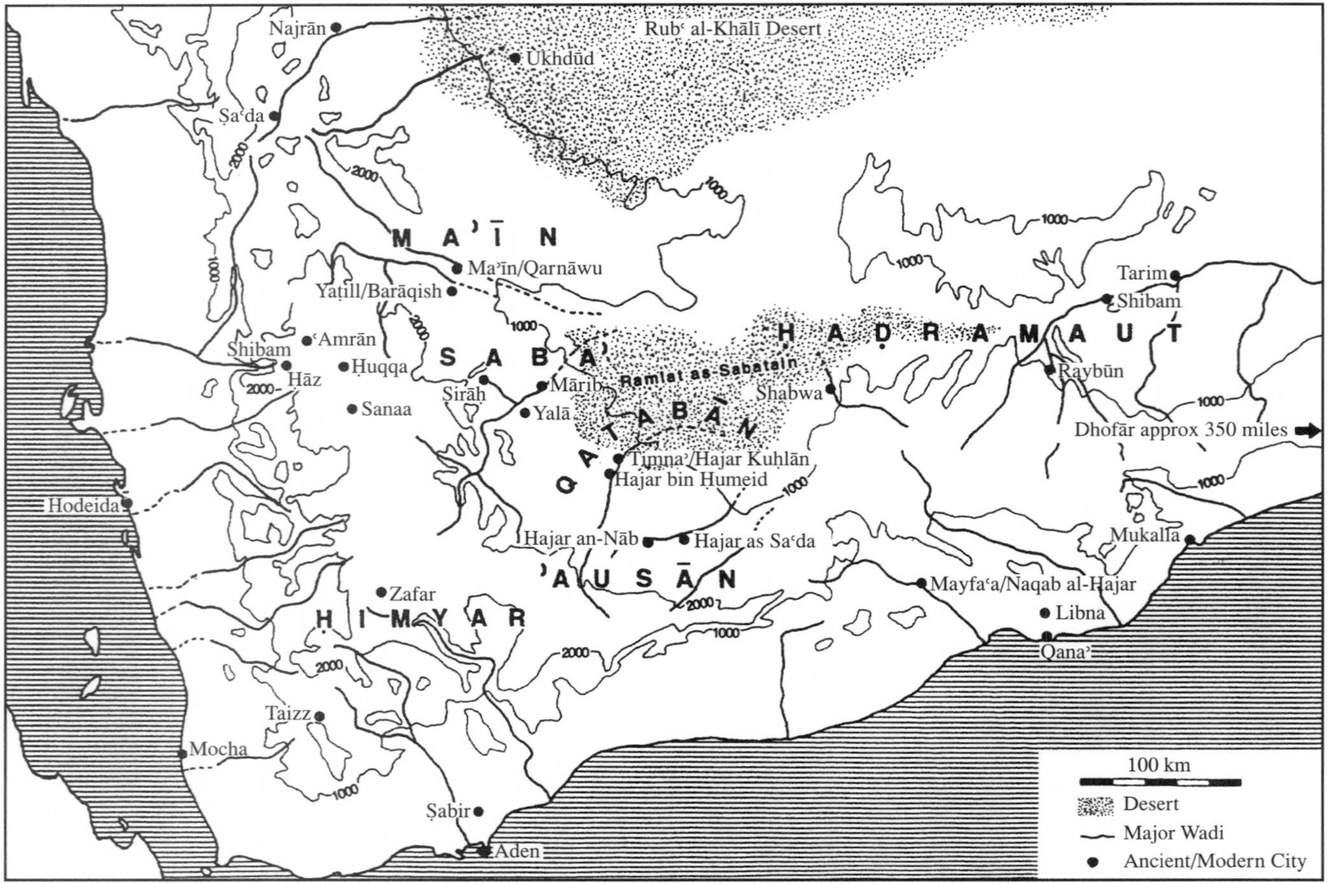
Rubʿ al-Khālī Desert
Najrān
Ukhdūd
Ṣaʿda
MAʾĪN
Maʾīn/Qarnāwu
Yaṭill/Barāqish
ʿAmrān
Shibam
Ḥāz
Ḥuqqa
Sanaa
SABAʾ
Ṣirāḥ
Mārib
Yalā
Ramlat as Sabatain
QATABĀN
Timnaʿ/Hajar Kuḥlān
Hajar bin Ḥumeid
HAḌRAMAUT
Tarim
Shibam
Raybūn
Shabwa
Dhofār approx 350 miles
Hodeida
Hajar an-Nāb
Hajar as Saʿda
ʾAUSĀN
Zafar
ḤIMYAR
Mukalla
Mayfaʿa/Naqab al-Hajar
Libna
Qanaʾ
Taizz
Mocha
Ṣabir
Aden
100 km
Desert
Major Wadi
Ancient/Modern City

Introduction

After my previous endeavors to offer a survey of the history, archaeology, and art of the Parthians and the Sasanids in two small volumes, I intend now to present the history of ancient South Arabia in the same fashion. Whereas the Sasanids were relatively well known in both ancient sources and contemporary research, the situation we are presently faced with resembles more that of the examination of the Parthians; in other words, very little is known on the subject.

Many of us have certainly heard of the encounter between the Queen of Sheba and King Solomon, but who knows anything precise about the region this queen came from? Arabia, the largest peninsula in the world, covering over 1.4 million square miles—a quarter of the total land area of Europe—is still more or less unknown territory, the exploration of which is only in its beginnings. This also applies to the actual region of South Arabia, the area of the countries of North and South Yemen, which were united in 1990, covering almost 204,000 sq. mi. There are several reasons for our relative lack of knowledge. Archaeological field research, which provides the "raw materials" for further investigation, concentrated mainly on Mesopotamia, Iran, and Anatolia for a long time—that is, from the very beginning of archaeological exploration of the Middle East in the mid-nineteenth century until after the end of World War II. In addition, political problems later complicated the situation, such as the existence of two states, North and South Yemen, that were not very well disposed toward each other, and last but not least the civil wars in each of the two countries themselves. In 1994, just four years after the achievement of so-called unification, the two former partial states are fighting each other bitterly. Finally, the inaccessibility of the region and the somewhat hostile attitudes of the inhabitants toward the research efforts have served as hindering factors as well.

These reasons, to be sure, also led to the fact that although there were a lot of individual investigations, especially as regards language, very few general surveys have been conducted on the history, archaeology, and art of this region. An important step in this direction was definitely the excellent Yemen exhibition in 1987 in Munich and the catalogue to that exhibition, which included many interesting and significant articles. This small book is certainly not intended as a "competing project." Instead, it is merely an attempt to offer a consolidated overview of the current state of knowledge on the abovementioned topics. Not intended for specialists in research on Arabia, it is meant for laypeople interested in the subject, for Orientalists and historians of Ancient History who are not concerned exclusively with ancient South Arabia, and, finally, it will also be of interest to students of archaeology or the Ancient Orient.

For the English edition, two years after the publication of the German edition, I have corrected some errors, whether having discovered them on my own or having been made aware of them through reviews. I would especially like to thank my colleague Brent Shaw for his careful reading of the manuscript and his valuable scholarly suggestions for improving the English-language edition. In addition, some findings in recent literature have been integrated. In this context, the Yemen exhibitions in Paris, Vienna, and currently in Munich deserve special mention. I was able to draw from the Vienna catalogue *Jemen. Kunst und Archäologie im Land der Königin von Saba'* (1998). This is a revised and largely newly conceived version of the Paris catalogue, *Yemen au pays de la reine de Saba'* (1997). Although the Munich exhibition has already opened, as of July 1999 the catalogue has not yet become available. In contrast to the 1987 Yemen exhibition in Munich, this one is purely archaeological in nature.

Finally, it should be mentioned that in contrast to the German edition, names of persons and places in this English translation have been transcribed according to common spelling conventions. Epigraphists might not be pleased with this practice, but I hope they will forgive me. And last but not least, I would like to thank my efficient translator Allison Brown.

Klaus Schippmann, Göttingen

I. Geography and Sources

It is not easy to define the terms "Arab"[1] and "Arabia," since their meaning changed considerably in the course of history. The earliest mention in Assyrian sources can be found on the famous monolith of Shalmanassar III (859-824). Here he reported on the battle of Qarkar in the Orontes Valley in 853 B.C., mentioning a member of the enemy coalition, a "Gindibu, the Arab," who took part in the battle with 1000 camels.[2] There was no other Assyrian mention of Arabs until the year 738 B.C., when Tiglath Pileser III (746-726) made a record in his annals about a queen of the Arabs named Zabība, who belonged to the enemy alliance that had been defeated by the Assyrian king and made to pay tribute. Additional mention of Arabs continues up to Assurbanipal (669-627/626).[3] His inscriptions reveal, however, that by this time names and other details about nomadic groups were used and no longer merely the general term "Arabs."[4] The earliest Biblical reference to "Arabs" that can be dated is in the Book of Isaiah (13:20), placing it in the second half of the eighth century B.C..[5]

The only information offered by the sources mentioned here is that there were nomads referred to as Arabs in the area of Syria-Palestine, especially in the desert, that is, in the northern part of the Arabian peninsula. In South Arabian sources, regardless of the chronology used,[6] Arabs do not appear until the first century A.D.[7] During this period, Pliny[8] too understood Arabia to be the region extending from the Amanus mountain range in the north to South Arabia in the south. According to this interpretation, Syria and Mesopotamia were also part of Arabia. A. Grohmann,[9] however, is correct in maintaining that such a definition is of little use with respect to the history of civilization and he falls back on the Arabic expression "Djazīrat al-ʿArab," "the island of the Arabs." By that he means the peninsula between the Red Sea, the Gulf of Aden, the Arabia Sea, and the Persian Gulf. The northwest boundary of this peninsula is unclear. Grohmann draws it from the Jordan valley, along the mountain ridge from Damascus to south of Palmyra to the Euphrates. He does not consider the well-known towns of Palmyra and Petra, since despite their Arab populations they were more part of Syrian-Aramaic culture. G. Rentz,[10] however, does not draw the boundary as far to the north. He sees the northern extension of the peninsula as reaching only as far as the borders separating Saudi Arabia and Kuwait from Jordan and Iraq. According to Rentz, the northernmost point is the town of ʿUnāza. This would mean that the Arabian peninsula is about 1400 mi. (2200 km) long and 750 mi. (1200 km) wide, covering well over a million square miles. About one-fifth of this huge territory is desert—the largest sandy desert in the world, the Rubʿ al-Khālī, covering about 200,000 square miles, and the an-Nafūd desert, almost 30,000 square miles in size.

In ancient times since Ptolemy[11] (second century A.D.), Arabia was divided into three zones: Arabia Petraea, Arabia Deserta, and Arabia Felix. The first referred to the area in the Roman sphere of influence, with Petra (Jordan) as its center and including the Sinai peninsula as well. Arabia Deserta comprised mainly the Syrian-Mesopotamian desert, bordering on Arabia Petraea in the west. It was separated from Arabia Felix in the south by a line that started somewhat south of Aqaba, running more or less directly eastward along the mountains, reaching the Persian-Arabian Gulf south of the mouth of the Euphrates.

According to today's political map, most of Saudi Arabia and Kuwait, as well as the United Arab Emirates, Yemen, and Oman, would correspond to Arabia Felix. However, if one considers the history of the various kingdoms of South Arabia, this geographical expanse appears too large. South Arabia included primarily Yemen (former South and North Yemen), Dhofār (Oman), and the region of Najrān and parts of the Hejaz (Saudi Arabia). In other words, in geographical terms one must speak of southwestern Arabia. This part of Arabia was significant mostly for various trade routes that ran from the south—approximately from the ports of Aden and Qanaʾ, and from Dhofār—to the Mediterranean (Gaza) and the Persian Gulf, especially Gerrha, and further on to Mesopotamia. One of these routes was the legendary incense route. Of course extensive trade also took place in the opposite direction, from the Mediterranean to the south and then continuing further by sea to India.[12]

This region is in the tropical zone and has, in contrast to other parts of Arabia, a favorable climate and is very fertile. It is one of the most densely populated areas in Arabia. Several[13] major landscapes can be distinguished. In the former North Yemen, and in South Arabia as well, the Tihāma ("Hot Earth") plain is a 30-45 mile wide piece of land in the west, i.e., along the Red Sea. It includes not only the sparcely populated coastal plain that rises to about 650 feet (coastal Tihāma), but also the adjacent hilly foothills (mountain Tihāma) with altitudes up to about 2500 feet. This merges directly into a steep mountainous region. These Yemen highlands, where the cultivation of coffee thrives, is the most favorable climatic zone. This region leads into the central highlands, with altitudes starting at about 6900 feet. Southwest of Sanaa is Hadur Shuaib, with a height of over 12,000 feet the highest peak on the Arabian peninsula. Here in the highlands is the watershed between the Red Sea and the Arabian deserts in the interior. These highlands merge into the arid inland plateau, where larger oases (such as Mārib) were situated in the valleys, irrigated by the *sayl* (flash floods of runoff that occasionally occurred, mostly in arid wadis). However, control of this massive flooding required a complex system of irrigation that could only be set up and maintained in collective operations.

Former South Yemen was also divided into several different major landscapes.[14] Here too there is a coastal zone, though flat coasts alternate with steep ones. Aden, for example, is located in a double crater. The flat coastal strips have a depth of about 12-20 miles. Near Laḥej, north of Aden, the lowlands even reach a depth of 30 miles. Several large wadis open up access to the interior. Adjacent to the coastal zone is a mountainous region with peaks of up to 3300 feet, which

Tihāma (between Chocha and Zabil)

then merges into the "South Arabian plateau" with heights reaching about 6500 feet. Part of this zone in Ḥaḍramaut is formed by the jol, a barren limestone plateau. After crossing this plateau, one reaches the famous Wadi Ḥaḍramaut. It is located a little over 100 miles as the crow flies from the South Arabian coast, and extends parallel to the Gulf of Aden from west to east for 125 miles. Numerous tributaries from the north and south lead into Wadi Ḥaḍramaut, whereby it is mostly the southern valleys that bring the sayl, which makes the land fertile, and thus they are more densely populated.

Continuing to the north from Wadi Ḥaḍramaut, one arrives at the Ramlat Ṣayhad (Ramlat as-Sabʿatayn) desert in the northwest.[15] It extends from as far as Mārib in the west to the Ḥaḍramaut plateau in the east. In antiquity, the regions west, south, and east of the Ramlat Ṣayhad formed the political and cultural centers of South Arabia. Here were the centers of the kingdoms of Sabaʾ, Maʿīn, Ḥaḍramaut, Qatabān, and probably also that of ʾAusān.[16]

North of the Ramlat Ṣayhad is the endless desert, Rubʿ al-Khālī, which extends into the interior of Arabia. The Mahra region, east of Ḥaḍramaut, makes up another major landscape of southern Yemen. Adjacent to the Mahra in the east is the Dhofār, which is politically part of present-day Oman, but in terms of geography and development belongs to southern Yemen. In ancient times, most of the incense came from the Dhofār.

With respect to climate, South Arabia can be divided into two major zones. A tropical, humid, unhealthy desert climate exists in the coastal zone and a similar climate, though with greater precipitation, is located in the adjacent lower slopes of the highland rim. The other, subtropical climatic zone exists in the higher altitudes of the rim, the highlands, and the oasis landscapes in eastern Yemen and the Ḥaḍramaut.[17]

II. The People

It is difficult to approximate today's population on the Arabian peninsula since reliable figures are lacking almost everywhere in the individual countries. As a result, statistics mentioned in various sources vary considerably. Former North Yemen provides an impressive example of this. The first population census was conducted there in February 1975. No reliable maps showing all settlements existed and some regions were accessible to the "election helpers" only through arduous, weeks-long foot marches. The census was carried out through the efforts of over 5000 secondary school and university students and government officials. Despite the problems cited, 96 percent of the population was believed to have been registered. Aided by aerial photograph interpretations and random sampling, a Swiss team of geographers determined the missing figures and checked the results for accuracy. The calculated number of 4.705 million residents living permanently in North Yemen is considerably lower than previous estimates, which spoke of a population of up to 9 million.[1]

A cautious figure for the two Yemenite states, Saudi Arabia, and Oman for 1975 is approximately 13 million permanent residents.[2] For both northern and southern Yemen alone, that is, the region corresponding basically to the territory of the ancient kingdoms of South Arabia, an estimated number of roughly 10 million residents was determined for 1984-86.[3] A census conducted at the end of 1994 yielded a figure of 15.9 million residents.[4] A portion of this total number of inhabitants of South Arabia is probably still nomadic bedouins.

Their total number can only be approximated, since the transition from full to semi-nomadism is difficult to identify precisely. Wohlfahrt[5] refers to a figure of two percent of the total population, whereby these statistics vary from country to country.[6]

Similar problems exist in determining the population of ancient South Arabia. It can be assumed that the oases back then were considerably larger than they are today. One reason for this is certainly the irrigation system, which continued to function well over many centuries. This means that the south, with its agricultural base, predominated over the desert lands in the north, which were inhabited mainly by bedouins.[7]

Figures relating to the population in ancient times are very rare in inscriptions or other sources, and modern-day research has also been very cautious in this regard. It must be kept in mind that numbers mentioned in inscriptions are only an indirect indication of population figures. They refer either to the number of enemies killed or prisoners taken[8]—whereby up to the present day victors always tend to exaggerate—or, for example, to the 20,000 people put to work to repair the Mārib dam in the year 450 A.D.[9] Similar problems exist regarding reports of the size and number of conquered cities and villages. A. F. L. Beeston[10] has also mentioned the difficulty in defining an "urban center" for South Arabia. Thus he expressed doubt whether Timnaʿ, the capital of Qatabān, or Qarnāwu, the capital of Maʿīn, would fall into this category. In fact, he maintained the view that there was no true urbanization at all in ancient South Arabia except for the port of Qanaʾ.

Nevertheless, some figures do exist for Mārib, the largest city in South Arabia. The Sanaa[11] department of the German Archaeological Institute reported that in their heyday (seventh and sixth centuries B.C.), the Sabaeans in Mārib had about 25,000 acres of fertile land at their disposal for cultivation. Since there were two harvests annually, the total area of cultivated land must be double that figure. According to Grohmann, the ancient city itself covered roughly 282 acres (114 hectares).[12]

In 1973 there were about 13,000 people living in the administrative district of Mārib (Qada), only 10,000 of whom were sedentary.

Mārib dam

They farmed an area of almost 10,000 acres.[13] If this ratio of cultivated land to inhabitants is applied to ancient times, it would mean that at least 30,000 people could have subsisted in Mārib.[14] U. Brunner has said that even if it is assumed that the land was farmed more intensively in antiquity, this could have provided for a maximum of only 50,000 people. He therefore considered a figure of 100,000, as claimed by C. Rathjens,[15] to be unrealistic. If we thus assume a population of 50,000 in the Mārib oasis, an additional roughly 30,000 for the environs of Mārib, and von Wissmann's[16] figure of 200,000 for the Samʿi territory (according to von Wissmann this included primarily the region west of Mārib, i.e., beyond Sanaa about as far as Kaukaban, and south beyond Ẓafār),[17] the total population figure is then approximately 280,000. The regions of Mārib and Samʿi made up the major part of the kingdom of Sabaʾ in terms of area. Even if another 30,000 people are generously added for the portion of the kingdom beyond Mārib and Samʿi, the result is roughly 310,000 inhabitants for the kingdom of Sabaʾ. I believe this figure could hardly have been exceeded by those for the kingdoms of Maʿin, ʾAusān, Qatabān, Ḥaḍramaut, and Ḥimyar, since according to today's knowledge an irrigation system as expansive and perfected as that of the Mārib oasis never existed in any of the other kingdoms. This was one of the main prerequisites for large population figures, so Mārib was by far the largest city in ancient South Arabia.[18] These "number games" must take into account the fact that the population figures for the other kingdoms cannot simply be added to the above-mentioned figure of 310,000 people, because the kingdom of Ḥimyar, which was powerful at the end of the ancient period in South Arabia, developed around 120 B.C. out of parts of the collapsed kingdom of Qatabān[19] and, together with Sabaʾ, comprised the primary force in South Arabia. Thus the population figures for the kingdom of Ḥimyar are also largely included within figures for the kingdom of Qatabān.

Using evaluations of satellite photographs of the wadis around the Ramlat Ṣayhad desert (present-day Ramlat as-Ṣabʿatayn), U. Brunner and H. Haefner[20] tried to calculate the expanse of the irrigated oases. They worked out a minimum oasis area of over 100,000 acres and a total of 200,000 people who lived at the periphery of the Ramlat

Mārib temple

Ṣayhad, i.e., in the region including the centers of the ancient kingdoms of South Arabia.

Summarizing, I am thus of the opinion that the population of ancient South Arabia, that is, the area of united Yemen, was at most half a million, as compared with today's figure of about 16 million people.[21] I believe this major difference can be explained by today's higher life expectancy as a result of medical care, the mechanization of agriculture, and the implementation of irrigation projects such as the one in the Tihāma.

For comparative purposes, the estimated sedentary population of the Indus civilization, which covers more than half a million square miles—compared with the roughly 200,000 square miles of united Yemen—was approximately 1 million people not including nomadic herders.[22]

There is also much disagreement among researchers regarding yet another question, namely, the ethnic origins of the people who lived in ancient South Arabia. In other words, did the people who inhabited this region after around 1000 B.C.—which marks the approximate beginning of the historical period we are presently concerned with—migrate there or was this an autochthonous population?

It has been determined that South Arabia was populated long before 1000 B.C.[23] This has been confirmed by numerous excavations,[24] especially those after 1945 in both Yemens,[25] Oman,[26] Bahrain, Saudi Arabia,[27] and the Emirates.[28] Generally, current research assumes that a migration to South Arabia—which is relevant to our study here—took place at the end of the third or beginning of the second millennium B.C. According to Grohmann[29] and von Wissmann,[30] it took place in the wake of movements to Syria and Mesopotamia from the north and east. In particular von Wissmann described this immigration more precisely, reporting[31] that "our" Sabaeans, Minaeans, Ḥaḍramites, and Qatabānians came from East Arabia, more specifically the area around present-day Bahrain, in several waves sometime during the second millennium B.C. The region around the Gulf of Bahrain, together with Bahrain Island—the ancient Dilmun, according to findings of, especially, Danish excavations since the early 1950s—had been an important commercial center for trade between Mesopotamia and the Indus valley since the early third millennium B.C. The legendary cities of Gerrha, Hajar, and Thaj were also located somewhere in this area. Recently it has even been assumed that all three names refer to one and the same city.[32]

However, whether one can speak of this region and its inhabitants as an "advanced civilization," as von Wissmann does, is another question. G. Garbini[33] makes a small distinction with respect to the migration. He said it was only the Minaeans, Qatabānians, and Ḥaḍramites who migrated to South Arabia in the second millennium B.C., the Sabaeans not having arrived until around 600 B.C.

One must concur with von Wissmann that these migrations were aided by the use of domesticized riding camels. His assumption[34] that camels were first bred around the middle of the second millennium B.C., however, is incorrect. The excavations on the Oman peninsula, especially the ones in Hili and on Umm an-Nar have shown that camels (dromedaries) were already being domesticized at the end of the fourth or the beginning of the third millennium B.C.[35] Thus the question must be posed if this migration to South Arabia might not have indeed taken place earlier, since access to the necessary means of transportation, the camel, had already been attained prior to the middle of the second millennium B.C.

The oldest ethnic group in this region, according to von Wissmann,[36] was the "South Arabians." They could be found in particular among semi-nomadic tribes of the mountain range at the edge of the Ḥaḍramaut and they resembled the Veddas of India. Also according to von Wissmann, the Gonds[37] spread out from along the Indian coast to South Arabia. Von Wissmann reported that they live primarily in the Deccan in India, and in the Tihāma, that is, along the Red Sea coast, in the Yemen highlands, the Ḥaḍramaut, and the Dhofār. Ethiopians,[38] related to the European people, also originally came from India (northwest India) and moved northwestwards at a very early time. In South Arabia, they live in the interior, from the eastern slopes of Yemen to the Ḥaḍramaut to the Qara mountains in the Dhofār. Inland movements from the north are indicated by oval-faced Mediterranean and Oriental peoples. Based on body and facial shape, north European oval-faced peoples also inhabit the area. Among

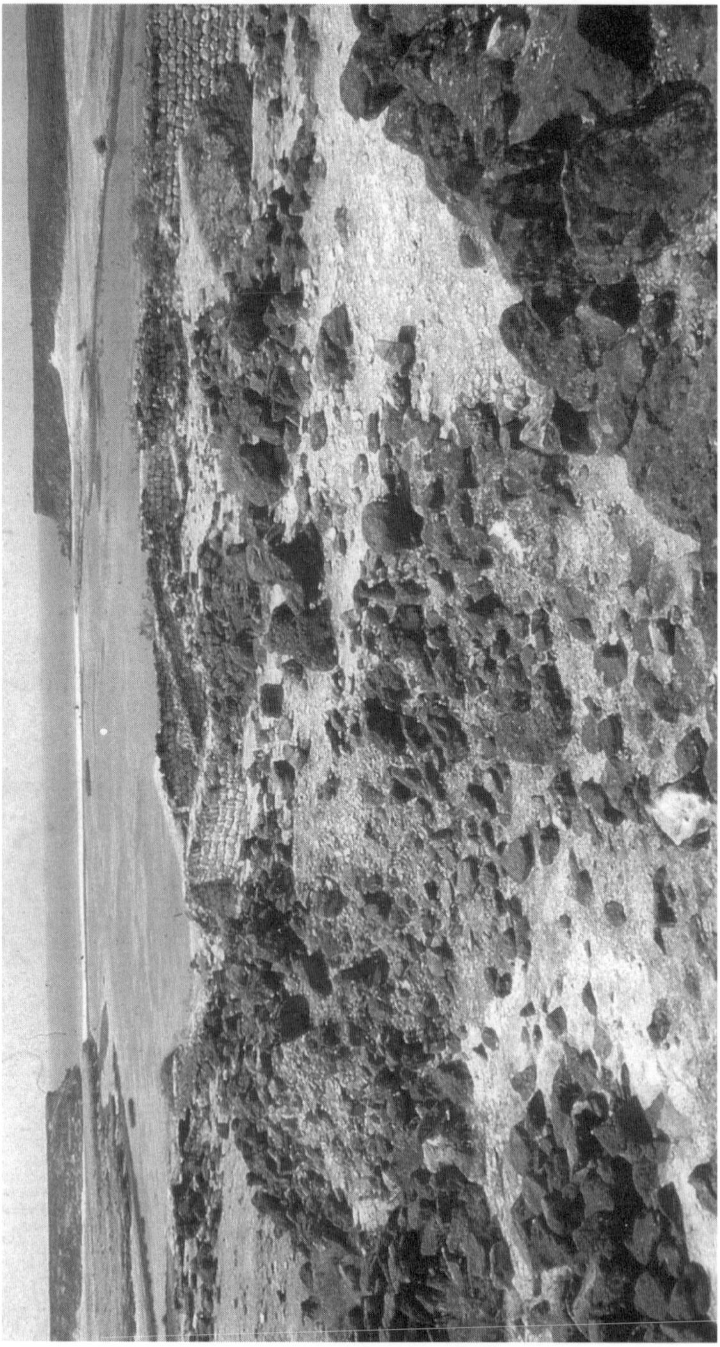

Sumhurow

some tribes in northern Yemen, as much as 8-12 percent of the population was found to be blond and blue-eyed.

Finally, as regards ethnic groups in South Arabia, particularly in Yemen, field researchers have found that a strong racial mixture of peoples existed as early as the beginning of the first millennium B.C. Grohmann[39] referred to a "mixed zone," which would indicate that many migrations took place, the most significant of which were probably from the north and east.

There is hope that, in joint efforts, archaeologists and anthropologists find enough material in future excavations to offer further insight into the different populations of South Arabia throughout the millennia.[40]

III. Languages and Writing

This chapter will begin to shed light on the difficult and tedious path yet to be taken by research in offering a more or less comprehensible view of languages and writing in ancient South Arabia. The difficulties facing linguistic scholars are apparent, for example, in the fact that totally different translations sometimes exist for one and the same inscription. This is perhaps surpassed only by the discrepancy in views of scholars regarding the chronology of ancient South Arabia.

The Old South Arabic language is known to us only through extant inscriptions. It belongs to the family of semitic languages[1] and displays similarities to Abyssinian languages as well as Accadian-Babylonian.[2]

Until recently, Old South Arabic was known only from monument inscriptions, which meant that our knowledge of this language was as limited as the content of these inscriptions. Religious inscriptions are very important in this regard; in addition, building inscriptions, laws, contracts, and gravestone inscriptions also exist. The style of these inscriptions is very rigid and uniform. Maria Höfner[3] has spoken of a style that "has been frozen almost to the point of being stereotyped set phrases." With few exceptions, speech is always in the third person; first and second person appear very rarely. In over 5000 published texts, for example, there are less than a dozen examples of speech in the second person.[4]

The length of the inscriptions varies greatly; some known inscriptions contain only several words while others have up to one thousand. The writing itself is impressive in its linearity and clarity. Some inscriptions, especially those from the early period, were written in boustrophedon form, that is, "turning as the ox plows," in alternating directions as furrows are dug. Later the direction of writing was generally from right to left. There were twenty-nine letters in the Old South Arabic alphabet. What did the spoken language sound like? Here we can only speculate, since there were no vowel signs.

Several years ago, a totally different type of inscription was discovered: small wooden cylinders written on with a type of stylus. What was new and significant is that the writing was in a form of cursive handwriting. It was used to record events of daily life such as letters, contracts,[5] etc. This writing was in lower case, corresponding to our small print letters, whereas the monument inscriptions were written in large capitals. These more recent finds contain many new, unfamiliar words, so that it will probably take quite a long time to decipher them entirely.[6] One thing that stands out in these inscriptions is that first and second person are also used.

Up to now I have spoken of "Old South Arabic," but actually this is not specific enough. Rather, four dialects are known: Minaic, Qatabānic, Ḥaḍramitic, and Sabaic. The first three mentioned form a group, the so-called s-languages, as compared with Sabaic, which is an h-language. This characterization denotes the first phoneme of the pronominal suffix. More recently they have been referred to not as different dialects[7] but as four separate languages. A. F. L. Beeston[8] supported their being considered languages because they clearly differ from one another. However, he has admitted that this question cannot be answered definitively since the short vowels of these languages are not known.

Nevertheless, he has suggested a different term for these languages. According to Beeston it must be assumed—even though definitive evidence is lacking—that the Ḥimyarites also had their own, non-Sabaic language. He especially stressed that three inscriptions are now known that were written in an unknown language, and that it is thus helpful to define the four known Old South Arabic languages more precisely to distinguish them from other Old South

Arabic language forms. Since, according to Beeston, the centers of the Minaean, Sabaean, and Qatabānian kingdoms, and even Shabwa, the former capital of Ḥaḍramaut, were all located at the periphery of the Ramlat Ṣayhad (present-day Ramlat as-Ṣabʿatayn) desert, he has suggested the term "Ṣayhadic."

As regards the quantity of Ṣayhadic inscriptions, the largest number of them are Sabaic. This is most likely the reason why not one, but two Sabaic dictionaries appeared in 1982.[9] A distant second and third in number are Minaean and Qatabānian texts, though it is interesting that the former can also be found in Egypt and on the Greek island of Delos. This can be explained by the fact that the Minaeans carried on trade worldwide. Ḥaḍramitic texts are least known.

In this context, I would like to mention briefly the "discovery" of the alphabet, a subject of heated debate among researchers for many years. Fuel was added to the discussion especially after the discovery of the famous alphabet tablets at the excavations in Ras Shamra (Syria) at the ancient site of Ugarit. At question was primarily the development of the Northern and Southern Semitic alphabet tradition.[10] Which is historically older? This question remains disputed to today.[11] According to Jacqueline Pirenne,[12] the alphabet appeared in the tenth century, B.C. in Phoenicia, whereas the Old South Arabic alphabet came much later, in the fifth century B.C. William F. Albright,[13] however, has found this derivation to be implausible. He and other scholars[14] have maintained that the South Arabic alphabet developed from one of the many proto-Canaanite alphabets whereas, based on its dating in the fourteenth century B.C., the Ugarit alphabet can be viewed as the oldest piece of evidence. They have also suggested that the South Arabic alphabet did not break from the northern branch any later than the thirteenth century B.C. In A. G. Lundin's[15] view, the Phoenician alphabet was a derivitive of the Ugarit. Lundin also assumed that the alphabet "was created in a unique act around 1500 B.C. in the Semitic realm in Palestine, Phoenicia, Syria," and that from this common base, two branches developed, the Northern and the Southern Semitic. The earliest sample of a Southern Semitic alphabet, according to Lundin, is the clay tablet of Beth Shemesh, in Palestine, which he dated in the thirteenth century B.C.[16] J. Ryckmans[17] also assumed that the two alphabet traditions have a common source, though the origin of these Semitic alphabets is part of a longer and diverse process. These "alphabet families" are older than the Ugarit alphabet, according to Ryckmans, and should be dated in the first half of the second millennium B.C. These are the opinions of several authoritative Sabaean scholars; the list of differing opinions could be continued ad infinitum.

IV. Exploration History

Knowledge of Yemen had been very limited in Europe until the mid-eighteenth century.[1] Portuguese fleets were one of the ruling powers in the Red Sea, Gulf of Aden, and the Arabian Sea in the sixteenth century, but other than reports on the coastal regions the Portuguese did not serve to further knowledge about Yemen at that time in Europe.

The first European to travel in Yemen and leave a record of his journey was the Italian Lodovico di Varthema of Bologna. He landed in Aden in 1504. As a Christian he was taken captive, though he was able to visit the cities of Sanaa, Taizz, and Aden. His report did not offer much material valuable for research, however. In 1712, de la Grelaudière, of France, traveled for a short time in northern Yemen.

The first research expedition that yielded really useful findings, though four of the five participants died in the process, was a Danish undertaking. The impetus for the journey, however, came from a German from Göttingen, Johann David Michaelis (1717-1791). I taught Middle Eastern archaeology in the Michaelis House, named after him, for twenty-five years. Michaelis characterized South Arabia as one of the strangest countries on earth and he hoped that its exploration would provide important insight especially for Biblical studies. On his initiative, the Danish royal court, above all Count Bernstorf, arranged an expedition that departed Europe in 1761, spending about a year in Egypt and arriving in Yemen at the end of December 1762, where it remained until August 1763. Carsten Niebuhr returned to his homeland in November 1767 as the sole survivor. Interesting and unusual about this expedition in the mid-eighteenth century was the fact that the participants came from a wide variety of scientific fields. Carsten Niebuhr was an engineer; F. C. von Haven was a philologist; C. Cramer, a physician; P. Forskäl, a botanist; and G. G. Baurenfeind, a painter. Niebuhr was probably the first European to view an Old South Arabic inscription in Mocha. The findings of this extended journey were recorded by Niebuhr in his famous three-volume work *Reisebeschreibung nach Arabien und anderen umliegenden Ländern* (Description of a Journey to Arabia and Other Adjacent Lands).

In 1811, the text of several small inscription fragments were published in Vienna. These had been viewed by Ulrich Jasper von Seetzen, a German, a year earlier in Yemen. He paid for this "fame," however, with his life in the year of publication. J. R. Wellstedt, C. J. Cruttenden, and J. G. Hulton, all English naval officers, were responsible for additional inscriptions becoming known in Europe between 1834 and 1836. A Frenchman, Paul Emile Botta, was traveling in Yemen in 1837 and "established" Middle Eastern archaeology five years later. He began digging in Niniveh in 1842. Although unsuccessful at that site, he enjoyed all the more success a short time later in Khorsabad, the late-Assyrian capital Dur-Sharrukin. In Yemen, though, he was a botanist and physician for Muhammad Ali, the viceroy of Egypt, who defeated the Wahhabis in the Hejaz for Sultan Salim.

In 1843 the German Adolf von Wrede explored the Ḥaḍramaut and was the first to report of a Ḥaḍramitic inscription. Unfortunately, his reports were not published until considerably later, since von Wrede was regarded as a swindler during his lifetime and his reports had been dismissed as fabrications. They were finally published in 1870 by H. von Maltzan, who himself rendered outstanding services to the exploration of South Arabia.

As a curiosity it should be mentioned that around 1859 a South Arabic inscription was found in the Sumerian metropolis of Uruk in southern Mesopotamia. It is now on display in the British Museum. In the early 1860s in Aden, the English colonel Coghlan obtained approximately forty small bronze tablets with South Arabic inscriptions, which had been found during house construction in ʿAmrān, a town north of Sanaa. Unfortunately, only the most well-preserved tablets were sent to Aden; the other, less well-preserved ones were melted down. These small tablets can also be admired in the British Museum.

The most significant epoch for the study of Old South Arabic inscriptions began in 1843, the same year as von Wrede's journeys, with the bold and successful trips taken by T. J. Arnaud, a Frenchman, who like Botta was in the service of the Egyptian viceroy. Arnaud, a pharmacist, was the first European to visit the Sabaean capital of Mārib—unless he was preceded by Seetzen, but reliable information is lacking. This daring undertaking yielded fifty-six copies of South Arabic inscriptions. It is also remarkable that they were already published only two years later, in 1845.

Research in the field received a large thrust through the expeditions of the Frenchman Joseph Halévy, a Semitist. Commissioned by the Académie des Inscriptions et Belles-Lettres, he traveled through Yemen in 1869-70 in search of materials for the *Corpus Inscriptionum Semiticarum,* published by the Académie. In addition to Mārib he also visited Qarnāwu, capital of the Minaean kingdom, and Ṣirwāḥ, the first capital of the Sabaean kingdom before it was moved to Mārib. In all, he was able to copy 686 Sabaic and Minaic inscriptions.

We know of another twenty-two inscriptions thanks to the Austrian Siegfried Langer, who traveled from Hodeida to Sanaa in 1882. A short time later, however, Langer was murdered while attempting to penetrate into the interior from Aden. The year 1882 marks a turning point and thus the beginning of a totally new epoch in the exciting history of research expeditions in South Arabia. From this point on, the Austrian Eduard Glaser has played an absolutely predominant role in Yemen research. On four extended expeditions between 1882 and 1894, he collected some 2000 Old South Arabic inscriptions, either as copies or rubbings. Glaser was the first in South Arabia to employ this method of using a brush and paper. He also acquired numerous inscription stones, reliefs, and other antiquities that are now located in museums throughout Europe.

With respect to the late nineteenth century the couple J. Theodore and Anna Bent should also be mentioned, who, among other things, copied a number of inscriptions in the Ḥaḍramaut.

One of the first scientists who took extensive photography equipment along on a Yemen expedition, and to whom we thus owe the first major photographic documentation of North Yemen, was Hermann Burchardt, a German. He traveled to Yemen for the first time in 1902. On his third expedition, in 1909, he was murdered along with his Italian colleague. His epigraphical materials have made their way to the State Museums in Berlin.

In 1908 a Minaeo-Graeco bilingual inscription was found on the Greek island of Delos.

World War I brought a break in the exploration of South Arabia. Not until 1927 did a new phase begin, with the expeditions of Carl Rathjens and Hermann von Wissmann. Although neither was an archaeologist or epigraphist—Rathjens was an anthropologist and von Wissmann a geographer—their expeditions yielded a large number of inscriptions. It is also significant that the two had official authorization to conduct the first systematic excavation in Yemen in 1928. They uncovered a Sabaean temple near al-Ḥuqqa, north of Sanaa. Together with the Dutch consul, D. van der Meulen, von Wissmann traveled throughout the Ḥaḍramaut in 1931. But not until 1934 did a German, Hans Helfritz, reach Shabwa, the capital of the ancient kingdom of Ḥaḍramaut, and even then it was only for one night and a few daytime hours. It is precisely this trip by Helfritz that was later referred to as "virtually fruitless for archaeological research,"[2] though it should be kept in mind that Helfritz conducted all of his numerous expeditions alone and without any great assistance.

Not only Europeans were involved in the exploration of South Arabia. Between 1926 and 1936, the Syrian Nazīh al-Muʾayyad al-ʿAzm conducted several expeditions in Yemen, which led him to Mārib and Ṣirwāḥ as well. To be sure, not being a European facilitated his travels. Another non-European expedition was sent from the University of Cairo in 1936. Although its main purpose was geological, geographical, and climatological, the expedition—with the assistance of M. Taufīq, S. A. Ḥuzayyin, and H. Y. Nāmī—nevertheless copied numerous inscriptions unknown up to then and even conducted two minor excavations in the Ḥaḍramaut.

St. John Philby, an Englishman known for his travels to Arabia, systematically examined the ruins of Shabwa in 1936. The two Englishwomen Gertrude W. Caton-Thompson and Freya Stark traveled in the Ḥaḍramaut in 1937-38. Under the leadership of Caton-Thompson, a temple of Sīn the Moon God was excavated in al-Ḥureiḍa in Wadi ʿAmd. The same year, English major R. A. B. Hamilton conducted a small excavation in Shabwa.

Between 1944 and 1945, M. Taufīq, an Egyptian, went to Yemen and visited Maʿīn, Yaṯill (present-day Barāqish) and other Minaean cities. Especially his photographs of Minaean structures and inscriptions served to advance the state of research. Another Egyptian, archaeologist Aḥmed Fakhrī, continued the undertakings of his compatriot in 1947, with considerable success. Above all his photographs of the Sabaic inscriptions at Mārib and Ṣirwāḥ were of very good quality. He also drew up reliable maps of various ancient sites.

There were a number of expeditions in the 1930s and 1940s, though a complete listing would go beyond the scope of this work. It shall suffice here to mention the English couple, W. Harold and Doreen Ingrams, and R. B. Serjeant.

In 1950 the largest archaeological project up to that time took place. The excavations were in and around Timnaʿ, capital of the ancient kingdom of Qatabān, in the former South Yemen. The enterprise was "organized," in the truest sense of the word, by the American Foundation for the Study of Man, founded expressly for this purpose by Wendell Phillips. Phillips, an American, was a mixture of adventurer, journalist, and researcher. He knew how to "sell" his undertakings well. To his credit, he was able to convince highly qualified scholars to take part, such as W. Foxwell Albright, A. Jamme, A. M. Honeyman, and R. Le Baron Bowen, to mention but a few. In addition to the excavations in Timnaʿ itself, extremely successful investigations were also carried out in the immediate and more remote vicinity. The entire project lasted until 1951. During the work in Timnaʿ, Phillips tried to obtain permission to excavate in

Mārib. Whereas Timnaʿ, in Wadi Beiḥān, was part of the British Aden Protectorate, Mārib, less than 40 miles away, was in the Kingdom of Yemen. The two countries did not have particularly friendly relations with each other.

Surprisingly, the Imam granted Phillips an excavation permit for Mārib in spring 1951. In December of the same year the excavation was commenced. The project had to be terminated suddenly in mid-February 1952 and all equipment and most of the finds were left behind. Members of the expedition fled to the neighboring Aden Protectorate. It remains unclear why the Imam, who was very hostile to foreigners, ever issued the excavation permit in the first place. Perhaps there were political motives; maybe it was believed that allowing an American expedition to enter the country could slow down the British influence in South Arabia. Phillips wrote a well-known book *Qataban and Sheba* (New York, 1955), which describes the excavations in Timnaʿ and Mārib, and especially all that went with it. If one is somewhat familiar with the Middle Eastern mentality, especially taking into account the situation in North Yemen at that time, the circumstances described in the book hardly seem surprising. It was not the first time that foreigners failed to sufficiently consider the attitudes of people living in that part of the world. Phillips evidently wanted to transform Mārib into a major archaeological "construction site"; among other things he planned to set up an airport in Mārib and demanded that numerous new roads be built.

Shortly after Phillips and his team were forced hastily to leave Mārib, an Egyptian mission entered the country, including H. Y. Nāmī, F. Sayyid and others. The researchers were allowed to go to Mārib, where they photographed numerous inscriptions.

Excavations took place at Khōr Rōrī, in Oman, in 1952-53, 1958, and 1962. Khōr Rōrī is the ancient Ḥaḍramitic harbor of Sumhuram.[3] Several inscriptions as well as a temple were discovered there. Andrew Williamson, an English archaeologist, died in 1974 when his vehicle drove over a landmine after he had made a few latex squeezes of inscriptions there.

From 1959 to 1960, the Englishman Lankester Harding conducted a systematic investigation and inventory of the ruins in the former

South Yemen, compiling his findings in *Archaeology in the Aden Protectorates,* a standard work published in 1964. Supplementing that book is Brian Doe's *Monuments of South Arabia* (1983).[4] Doe was a long-time director of the Department of Antiquities in Aden.

As of 1962, the civil war in northern Yemen and the unrest in the Aden Protectorate prevented any major scientific projects from taking place in Yemen for several years. Not until the 1970s, after two new countries were established—the Arab Republic of Yemen in the north and the Democratic People's Republic of Yemen in the south—did scientific interest in Yemen experience a revival. W. W. Müller, an epigraphist, W. Diem, an Arabist, and W. Radt, an archaeologist, made up a small German team that was invited to North Yemen in 1970 and allowed to travel throughout the country.[5] From 1971 to 1975 P. Costa, an Italian, was in government service in North Yemen as an archaeological advisor. He is to thank above all for the construction and reorganization of the national museum there.

Under the leadership of Jacqueline Pirenne, the French began excavating in Shabwa, the capital of the Ḥaḍramaut kingdom, in 1975. J.-F. Breton assumed the leadership in 1977.[6] The excavations continued until 1987. Starting in 1978, the French conducted a systematic investigation of Wadi Ḥaḍramaut. They discovered no less than nine temples.[7] The French also began conducting several surveys and excavations in North Yemen, in the district of al-Jauf and in the province of al-Bayḍā in 1978.[8]

The German archaeologist H. Hauptmann was commissioned by UNESCO to travel to North Yemen in early 1977 to advise the government there on archaeological projects and to help plan a new museum in Sanaa.[9] The German Archaeological Institute opened its Sanaa station in 1978, and J. Schmidt became its director.[10] The Institute conducted many important investigations, especially in the Mārib area. In the interest of demonstrating the "international" character of the expeditions, I must add, finally, that it was an Italian research group that conducted extensive surveys and excavations in the 1980s, studying the stone age in North Yemen.[11] The American Foundation for the Study of Man resumed its work in North Yemen from 1982 to 1985. Also requiring mention are the Soviet-Yemenite excavations in Ḥaḍramaut that began in 1972, especially in Qanaʾ and Raybūn.

Of course not all the researchers and expeditions that dealt with this region could be named here. Nevertheless, at the conclusion of this condensed survey of the history of research expeditions in South Arabia I would like to stress that this is the story of individuals who have left their mark on research on South Arabia: Niebuhr, Halévy, Glaser, von Wissmann, Rathjens, Fakhri, Caton-Thompson, Philby—to repeat but a few of them. It is strongly reminiscent of the early period of research on Mesopotamia. But the situation changed after the end of World War II. The "pioneer days" had come to an end and it was now well-organized, major expeditions that took center stage.

V. The History of South Arabia

1. THE PREHISTORIC PERIOD

For a very long time, not much was known of the archaeology in South Arabia during the prehistoric period. Today it seems somewhat strange that Yemen research concentrated almost exclusively on the relics of the ancient kingdoms of South Arabia, as if South Arabia had been a historical vacuum up to that time. Prehistoric archaeology started a little earlier in the former South Yemen than in the north. It was perhaps the political presence of the British in this region that facilitated the archaeological enterprises.

Gertrude Caton-Thompson conducted the excavation of the Moon Temple in Ḥureiḍa in 1938. That same year, also in Wadi Ḥaḍramaut, she discovered various groups of flint artifacts, three of which were from the Paleolithic Period and one from the Neolithic Period.[1] A survey lasting several months conducted by G. Lankester Harding in 1959-60 in the former Aden Protectorate should also be mentioned in this context.[2] And the survey of the Smithsonian Institute in Washington, D.C., carried out in 1961-62 under the leadership of G. W. Van Beek, provided extensive additional materials from the Paleolithic Period in Ḥaḍramaut.[3]

The Jabal Tala site in the province of Laḥej, about twelve miles north of the capital town of the same name, is, according to Brian Doe,[4] the oldest prehistoric site on Arabian soil. The tools found there, above all hand-axes, are of Acheulean manufacture, which Doe

al-Hajar al-Ghaimah (the standing stones)

dated at 450,000-300,000[5] years ago. He referred to these "'hand-axe' men" as the first South Arabians, whereby he left open the question as to their place of origin. Doe did not rule out that this "hand-axe technique [might have been] distributed by the movement of migrants southward on both sides of the Red Sea." An Italian-Yemenite team found similar hand-axes in 1983 on the Dhamār plain, a few miles south of the town of Ma'bar, in the former North Yemen.[6]

As already mentioned, early stone age research began later in North Yemen. G. Garbini[7] found obsidian tools near Bait Naᶜām, about 12 miles west of Sanaa, in 1969. These he cautiously dated as coming from the Middle Paleolithic Period.

Starting in the mid-1970s, South Arabia's prehistory was systematically studied by major missions, the most significant of which were conducted by the Italians and the French. A French expedition under the leadership of R. Bayle des Hermens spent two months in 1974 conducting a survey of North Yemen.[8] They located about twenty prehistoric sites, including some with rock paintings,[9] about ten tumuli, and some megalithic rock formations.[10] The French came to the conclusion that evidence of the Paleolithic Period was very rare, whereas the Neolithic Period could be identified much more frequently. There were regional differences, however. Thus the region around Mārib must be distinguished from the neolithic sites in the north near Sanaa. The same is true for the Tihāma regions at the Red Sea and the ones around Sanaa and Dhamār.

Since 1980 the Italians have completed several comprehensive surveys, especially in the former North Yemen, conducted in cooperation with the North Yemenites. Among others, some sites with artifacts from the Middle Paleolithic Period were discovered. The most significant of these are Humayd al-ᶜAyn in the region of Khaulān aṭ-Ṭiyāl[11] and, not far away, al-Masanna.[12] The even older site near Ma'bar has already been mentioned in connection with the site of Jabal Tala in South Yemen. In the course of the years that followed, the Italians were able to locate numerous other sites from a wide range of prehistoric periods up to the beginning of the historical age, that is, around 1000 B.C.[13]

More recent studies conducted by the American Foundation of the

Study of Man should also be mentioned. The foundation continued to remain active in Yemen even after the death of Wendell Phillips. A team worked from 1982 to 1985 along the incense route in Wadi al-Jūbah, halfway between Mārib and Timnaʿ, in the former North Yemen.[14] Their goal was to discover archaeological sites from all periods in this region, which had hardly been explored at all up to then. In addition to a few paleolithic artifacts, numerous sites from the Neolithic-Chalcolithic Period, from the fifth to the fourth millennium B.C., were discovered.

If an attempt is made to draw any conclusions from these and other surveys about the prehistoric periods in Yemen, it can at least be said that parts of this region were definitely inhabited during the Paleolithic Period. With regard to former North Yemen, this is especially true for the Yemenite highlands, the areas of the eastern foothills, and the valleys along the wadis in the Tihāma.[15] For former South Yemen, this applies mostly to the region around Wadi Ḥaḍramaut and the area south of the Jabal Tala, as well as the area around Shabwa.[16]

As previously mentioned, the largest prehistoric civilization in northern Yemen existed during the Neolithic Period, albeit with regional differences.[17] As yet, little evidence of the Neolithic Period has been discovered in former South Yemen. Again, it has been located primarily in Wadi Ḥaḍramaut.[18] Brian Doe also reported of neolithic artifacts being found in the area around Fort Habarūt,[19] some 180 miles east of Tarīm near the border to Dhofār, Oman. Finally, the region around Shabwa must also be mentioned again.[20]

It was possible to close the "gap" between the Neolithic and the Historical Periods due to the efforts of, above all, Italian expeditions that took place between 1981 and 1985 in the region of Khaulān aṭ-Ṭiyal, about 25-30 miles southeast of Sanaa.[21] It appears that this Bronze Age civilization in northern Yemen spanned the entire second millennium B.C. Also in this context are the artifacts found by the American expedition in Wadi al-Jūbah. The artifacts found at the Hajar at-Tamrah[22] site showed a C-14 dating of 1330 ± 110 B.C. (CCR = calibrated date 1850-1385 B.C.) for the undermost layers.

For the periods mentioned, research expeditions that were conducted in other parts of Arabia must also be taken into consideration. This includes the paleo- and neolithic discoveries in the large sandy desert of Rubᶜ al-Khālī (Saudi Arabia). In Oman, the United Arab Emirates, and Bahrain, surveys and excavations have also indicated relationships and connections to Yemen.[23]

Although there are still considerable gaps in our knowledge, today it can be said with certainty that history in South Arabia did not begin with the ancient South Arabian kingdoms, but that this area began to play an important role much earlier, especially as a bridge between Africa and Asia.

2. THE EARLY CHRONOLOGY OF SOUTH ARABIA AND THE RELATED PROBLEMS

The historically recordable chapter of the total history of South Arabia certainly contains more facts and is more graspable to interested readers than the periods treated in the previous section. The present section throws us into the middle of the difficulties inherent in research on this period in South Arabian history. This has to do with the question of absolute and relative chronologies. Compared with other countries of ancient Middle East, there have been relatively few excavations conducted in South Arabia and they have contributed very little toward the drawing up of an absolute chronology. Even the method of radioactive carbon (C-14) dating, otherwise very helpful and often used in determining absolute datings, has led to few results, since the level of error for the historical period is generally far too high.[24] Considering the fact that there is only one absolutely certain date in defining the Historical Period, namely, the campaign against the Sabaean kingdom led by the Romans under Aelius Gallus in the years 25-24 B.C., the difficulties are obvious.

For this reason, research on South Arabia has attempted to solve the problem of a chronology primarily on the basis of paleography, that is, the study of ancient writings and inscriptions, no matter what the material. Just as spoken language continues to evolve, so does the writing, so that it is possible to order the extant South Arabian inscriptions relative to one another.[25] H. von Wissmann and J. Pirenne, the two great antipodes in the field, refer, respectively, to "paleographic levels" and "periodes graphiques" or "stades graphiques."

But, and here is the crux of the matter, scholars are anything but agreed on even the relative chronological order of the various inscriptions. One need only look at the numerous articles that have appeared on the subject of chronology in the journal *Bibliotheca Orientalis* since 1953[26] to recognize the problem. Thus today, as in Mesopotamian archaeology,[27] there is mention of three different chronologies: the "Long," "Mixed," and "Short" Chronologies.[28] These three variants will be described below, followed by a few arguments containing the pros and cons of each. The oldest of the three is the "Long Chronology," which was first put forward by, above all, E. Glaser[29] and F. Hommel.[30] However, there are differing opinions as to the dating of the start of the "Long Chronology." Two Assyrian texts, among others, are referred to in explanation. In one, Sargon II reported in about 715 B.C. that Yiṯaʿʾamar of Sabaʾ had paid tribute, and somewhat later, around 685 B.C., there is a similar reference in Sanherib's annals, though here it was Karibilu of Sabaʾ who had supplied the gifts. These two names were believed to have been found in a major Sabaic inscription (Gl. 1703[31]), the so-called Great Genealogy, a genealogical listing of Sabaean rulers. The names in that listing were Yiṯaʿʾamar and Karibilu. However, since Hommel did not believe these two rulers came at the beginning of their ancestral line, he came up with the date 985 or at the latest 950 B.C. for the beginning of the so-called Mukarrib Period.[32] Hommel also believed that on the basis of inscriptions the kingdoms of Qatabān and Maʿīn were considerably older than Sabaʾ, beginning in the thirteenth century B.C. This latter theory has mostly been abandoned[33] and now it is generally accepted that Sabaʾ was the earliest kingdom in South Arabia. Hommel's dating of 985-950 B.C. for the beginning of the Mukarrib Period has also generally lost its acceptance among researchers who support the "Long Chronology." H. von Wissmann,[34] who can be regarded the "leader" of this group, maintained that the eighth century B.C. marks the start of the Mukarrib Period. It should also be mentioned that even Hommel[35] offered 815 B.C. as the start of the Mukarrib Period, provided that "two other mentions of a Yitamara and a Karib-ilu in close chronological succession were also possible for the Yiṯaʿʾamar and Karibilu determined through cuneiform inscriptions to be 715 and 685 B.C."

This dating, the eighth century B.C., is accepted, not only in "the German-speaking realm," as claimed by Pirenne,[36] but in other language realms as well, for example, by A. Jamme[37] and W. F. Albright.[38] J. Ryckmans changed his mind on the subject several times. In 1951[39] he set the beginning of the Mukarrib Period in the ninth century; in 1957[40] he supported the "Short Chronology" of Pirenne, and recently he has returned to the "Long Chronology."[41] The Russian scholar A. G. Lundin[42] went even further back in history and named the eleventh century B.C. as the starting date. A. F. L. Beeston assumed an intermediate position, naming the sixth century.[43]

The so-called "Mixed Chronology" was put forth by Pirenne. It was based primarily on the findings of the American excavations in Timnaʿ and surroundings, Hajar bin Ḥumeid, and Mārib. According to Pirenne, the findings as well as the conclusions drawn by the excavators confirm her theory of the origin of the kingdoms of Qatabān and Maʿīn, namely, that Sabaʾ was established earlier. But the American excavation team had adopted the "Hommel theory" of Sabaʾ's being established in the eighth century, i.e., the "Long Chronology," according to Pirenne, which she felt was incorrect.

In my view, the "Mixed Chronology" is irrelevant. The important thing is the dating of the beginning of the Mukarrib Period in Sabaʾ, that is, either the eighth century B.C.—ignoring for the moment the earlier datings—or the fifth century B.C. Debate on whether the kingdoms of Maʿīn and Qatabān ended in B.C.—as purported by Albright—or A.D.—according to Pirenne—has no great significance in my opinion.

Thus I believe that only two chronologies are true rivals, the long one, and the short one, as described in detail by Pirenne in her 1956 work *Paléographie des Inscriptions sud-arabes* and later modified and substantiated in subsequent works.[44] According to the "Short Chronology," the "beginning of the monumental civilization of Sabaʾ

and Maʿīn cannot be dated any earlier than the fifth century B.C."[45] Pirenne's main argument is based on paleography, though numismatic and art historical "evidence" is also used.

As previously mentioned, however, there is much controversy among scholars with respect to the paleographical interpretation of the inscriptions. Above and beyond this remains the fundamental question, to what extent can paleography truly help, that is, is it really an "all-purpose remedy"? In this context, I would like to refer to a review of Pirenne's *Paléographie des inscriptions* that was written by one of the "grand gentlemen" of research on South Arabia, Beeston,[46] in which he clearly explained the limits and problems of paleography.

Objections to the "Long Chronology," presented again and again by, above all, Pirenne, are that it is based on the assertion that South Arabian writing is alphabetical. Since it is "undisputed," according to Pirenne, that the alphabet first appeared in Phoenicia and was "usable" around the tenth century B.C., that should be regarded as a "fixed date in history." She claimed that the ancient South Arabian writing form developed in the fifth century B.C. from the Aramaic and Hebrew alphabets, which in turn were derived from the Phoenician alphabet, the alphabet of Dedān (northwestern Arabia), and the Greek alphabet. However, this basic thesis of Pirenne is by no means "undisputed."[47] As already mentioned, a theory also exists that the South-Semitic alphabet was derived from a proto-Canaanite alphabet via the Ugarit alphabet (14th century B.C.), and this branching occurred in the fourteenth or early thirteenth century B.C.[48] In fact, A. van den Branden[49] has claimed just the opposite is true, namely, that the Phoenician alphabet developed from a preliminary South-Semitic form.

A few years ago, J. Ryckmans[50] determined in connection with the Beth Shemesh alphabet tablet that Pirenne's theory is no longer tenable, since she failed to take into account the Ugarit alphabet (14th century B.C.), which was considerably older than the Phoenician alphabet (10th century B.C.) and which can be traced to an even earlier linear alphabet.

To close this discussion, a considerable difference of opinion exists among researchers today on the development and age of the

Old South Arabic alphabet. Only one of these views was put forth by the late Jacqueline Pirenne (though of course she had supporters[51]), no more and no less. On the other hand, this does not mean that the "Long Chronology" has thus been irrefutably proven.

Today, in keeping with Pirenne, the Assyrian synchronism of Hommel, that a Sabaean ruler named Karibilu sent presents to the Assyrian ruler Sanherib in 685 B.C., has often been rejected, even by W. F. Albright,[52] who otherwise supports the "Long Chronology." But this does nothing to change the fact that the Assyrian annals report that in 715 and 685 B.C., two Sabaean rulers gave presents or paid tribute. Another argument against the "Long Chronology" is a rejection of the assumption that the succession of the early Sabaean rulers was always a father to son succession, that is, that the fourteen known mukarribs relate to fourteen generations of rulers.[53] In Pirenne's view,[54] some of these rulers belonged to the same generation, but were in different branches of the ruling family. This would of course result in a shorter total span of time. Even if such an opinion is largely rejected, one can only agree with Beeston,[55] who said, "What grounds are there for thinking that a continuous direct father to son succession of the mkrb rulers of Sabaʾ is more likely than a succession often involving collateral lines? The reply can only be 'None'."

Another notion put forth by Pirenne[56] is that the "war between Media (Persia) and Egypt" mentioned in an inscription (RES 3022[57]) is one and the same as the campaign of Antiochos the Great against Ptolemy IV in 217 B.C. This might well be true, but the war could just as easily refer to the invasion of Egypt by the Persian king Artaxerxes in 343 B.C., as is often assumed.[58] The later dating should also be rejected, according to von Wissmann,[59] because the Seleucids were never characterized as "Medians." But most of all, Pirenne's dating became doubtful when she set her paleographic level E, which in her view included inscription RES 3022, before level D. Von Wissmann reported that Pirenne notified him of this correction in a letter. According to her own dating system, level D covered the period from roughly 300 to 250 B.C. and level C from 350 to 300 B.C. In other words, if RES 3022 were now assigned to level C, it would make the dating of 215 impossible; instead, the year 343 B.C. would be more likely.

In the end, it all depends on the paleographic interpretation by the respective scientist viewing an inscription. Interpretations vary to such a great extent, however, that I believe paleography, the method used by Pirenne, can only be used as a last resort. Beeston has described how he tried to grasp the procedure Pirenne suggested for graphic interpretation and assignment of the inscriptions to the levels A-E she defined. He was not able to do this or he did not come up with the same level assignment as Pirenne has suggested, he admitted frankly.

One must also note that one of the most significant inscriptions, the so-called Great Genealogy or Great Complex (Gl 1703), which was discovered by E. Glaser's team and which is the basis for parts of various chronologies suggested by different scientists, was not rediscovered until 1975. Until that time it was assumed that the site with the inscriptions was located in the vicinity of Ṣirwāḥ.[60] The rubbings were not made by Glaser himself; instead, he had taught the procedure to members of the native population, who then traveled around collecting inscriptions for him. They were sent to Glaser in Munich after the end of his fourth expedition to Arabia in 1892-94, apparently in three series. Glaser himself made only vague comments as to the sites where they were found. He referred either to an "unknown origin" or "probably from Ṣirwāḥ." As we now know, the rubbings made from the inscriptions were either incomplete or contained errors. Nevertheless, they were used extensively to re-create part of the succession of Sabaean rulers. Not until 1975, that is, eighty years later, was A. Jamme able to relocate the site and a short time later, in 1976, C. Robin visited the site where the inscriptions had been found. It is approximately 12 miles south of Mārib near Sawwana. It turned out that two different rocks were involved. After reliable rubbings and photographs were made, it could then be understood in retrospect that many of the readings that had been conducted over the previous eighty years were incorrect. But to today discourse continues on the correct reading of the inscriptions on these two rocks.[61] That should suffice here on the status and significance of paleography within Sabaean studies.

Objections to the "Long Chronology" are not only paleographic in nature, even if those are the primary ones. Pirenne compared Sabaean coins with the Attic drachm with an owl[62] from the fifth century B.C. According to Pirenne, imitations of this coin were made around the middle of the fourth century B.C. everywhere from the Middle East to India. Pirenne did not think the rulers in Saba᾿ could have made similar coins in the eighth century B.C., that is, three centuries before the Athenian prototype was created. But she did find it unthinkable that the magnificant civilization of the mukarribs existed for three or four centuries without currency and coin circulation. Even if one assumes that this dating is correct,[63] the decisive question is why it should be unthinkable that the Sabaeans could have existed economically and culturally prior to the sixth-fifth centuries B.C. without coins, that is, without money? There were many civilizations, some of which were considerably larger kingdoms than Saba᾿, that experienced magnificent cultural achievements yet lacked coins, among them the Egyptians, Assyrians, Babylonians, and even the Greeks (Mycenaeans) and Cretans. Furthermore, there was by no means a total "void" before coins. The coin represented only one of numerous, albeit less efficient, money forms. Then and earlier, currency also existed in the form of bartered goods, metal, tools, and bullion, to name only the most important ones used before the coin was "invented" in the seventh century B.C. in Lydia.[64] It is thus indeed possible that a Sabaean society without coin circulation existed prior to the fifth century B.C.

Another argument against the "Long Chronology" is explained by Pirenne on the basis of Sabaean architecture, or more precisely, its implementation: the masonry.[65] In Pirenne's view, the great architectural evidence of the Sabaean mukarribs was comparable to Persian (Achaemenian), Phoenician, and Greek architecture of the fifth century B.C. This shall not be disputed in principle, but these three "architectural regions" had predecessors, and it is with these predecessors that the stone building methods used in Mārib should be compared. G. W. Van Beek[66] and G. R. H. Wright[67] have mentioned the masonry of the middle of the Iron Age (tenth to eight centuries B.C.), for example, in Samaria, Megiddo, and Beth-shan, or the stone work at Ugarit (thirteenth century B.C.). A transition or rather an improvement in the method of making stone blocks took place in Assyria in the first half of the seventh century. The new technique was marginally drafted, pecked masonry, which corresponded to the masonwork used on many structures in Mārib. Pirenne's information,[68] as reported by E. Glaser and A. Fakhrī, that the large stone blocks in the Mārib dam were joined with metal clamps is only partially correct. A more recent investigation by G. R. H. Wright[69] clearly distinguishes between an older technique without metal clamps and a later one with them. The important thing, however, is that the conclusion drawn on the basis of the use of metal clamps,[70] that is, that this was not a practice before the end of the sixth century B.C. and thus construction of the Mārib dam was not started prior to this time,[71] is false—elsewhere Pirenne spoke of the fourth century B.C.[72] This method was used as early as in the "ancient kingdom" of Egypt (third millennium B.C.),[73] the Hittite kingdom, and in Mesopotamia and other regions. Finally, Pirenne brought up works of art, especially sculptures, that were found in South Arabia to support her argument against the "Long Chronology." She maintained that most of them can be traced back to Persian, Greek, or Palmyrene influence, which would mean they are more recent than the sixth century B.C.[74] Pirenne's[75] justification was based primarily, once again, on paleography: "Si l'on accepte les résultats acquis par notre 'Paléographie' [this is a reference to her book], on constatera que le type de statuette auquel appartient notre Yaṣdouq'il n'apparaît que vers 200 avant notre ère." In my view, Almut Hauptmann–von Gladiss[76] was not incorrect in writing, in her fundamental essay on the problems of ancient South Arabian sculpture ("Probleme alt-südarabischer Plastik"):

> Since the basic inscription [on a Qatabānian statuette] has been lost, we must exclude for now the problem of dating on the basis of the paleographic phases as developed by Pirenne, in which the beginning of standing prototypes had been fixed to a statuette in Paris as the turn of the third to the second century B.C., without any understanding of the form.

It can and should not be argued in principle that the influences mentioned by Pirenne have been documented in South Arabian art. But what does that prove? Only that works of art existed in this region that were created later than the sixth century B.C. This does not, however, justify dating the Mukarrib Period as starting after the sixth century B.C. Moreover, Pirenne overemphasized the Greek influence, as clearly demonstrated in her book *La Grèce et Saba.*

It must also be kept in mind that there are many gaps in the history of sculpture in South Arabia. The impression we have today is based mainly on finds made at only a small number of excavations. It is unclear whether many pieces are imports or indigenous. And here too, chronological questions are very significant and there is much disagreement. K. Parlasca[77] has reminded us that the dating of the famous bronze horse in the Dumbarton Oaks Collection in Washington, D.C. varies from the sixth-fifth century B.C. to the fifth-sixth century A.D.! He also reported that archaeological evidence of relations with the Mediterranean area extends "clearly" into the archaic period, that is, the seventh-sixth century B.C.[78] Parlasca mentioned South Arabia's relations to its neighbors to the north and northwest, such as Egypt. Almut Hauptmann–von Gladiss[79] and E. Will[80] also stressed the significance of Syria for South Arabian art. Despite these different external influences, it should not be forgotten that ancient South Arabian art definitely also has its own typical style. As examples, Hauptmann–von Gladiss[81] mentioned the alabaster heads in the Berlin Museum for Islamic Art.

To close discussion of paleography and the problems associated with it for now—we shall continue to deal with it later in this book—it can be summarized that clear and sufficient convincing evidence exists neither for the "Long" nor the "Short" Chronology, although I believe the scales are tipped in favor of the "Long Chronology." Jacqueline Pirenne certainly provided "comprehensive" discussion on "her" chronology, but the mainstay of her evidence, paleography, is a tool of the trade that allows too many different interpretations or datings of the respective inscriptions.

One must thus decide on one of the two chronologies. In the explanations that follow, I shall base my datings on the "Long

Chronology." As one justification, it has been determined definitively that the Assyrian sources mention Sabaean rulers in the years 715 and 685 B.C. Even if one assumes that they might not be the same Sabaean mukarribs as the ones named by Hommel and other scholars and documented in inscriptions, it cannot be denied that there were Sabaean rulers two centuries before Pirenne's fifth century dating. Perhaps the institution of mukarrib had not yet been established. How would advocates of the "Short Chronology" characterize this period: as "proto-Sabaean" or "pre-mukarrib"?

Pirenne[82] treated this in an "aperçu sur les temps antérieurs." She did not deny that Assyrian annals refer to Sabaean kings, and she listed this as the first point to be used in determining a South Arabian chronology. However, she qualified this statement by declaring that the kings were all from a single, however powerful, tribe. Discourse is thus geared to recognizing only those rulers characterized as mukarribs in the inscriptions as being relevant for Sabaean history. I consider this incorrect, if not illogical. There have been enough examples in history of great states whose rulers had different titles over the course of time; it can and should not be said that the history of the historical kingdom of Saba' did not begin until the start of the Mukarrib Period. Aside from that, Pirenne's opinion is decidedly linked to her paleographic-based dating of the two rulers named in the Assyrian annals.

I do not think it is of great import which "paleographic camp"—Pirenne or von Wissmann and their respective supporters—will one day turn out to be "right," and even then, determined primarily on the basis of archaeological finds and corresponding C-14 data. It is much more important to see the Historical Period of Saba' as a whole that began a few centuries earlier than the fifth century B.C. I believe that A. de Maigret[83] has correctly criticized the early scientific investigations of South Arabian civilization, claiming they concentrated above all on the inscriptions, though these offered at most a partial view. The inscriptions revealed nothing—either directly or indirectly—to explain the sudden emergence of the South Arabian states. Here I would like emphasize that I do not view the study of inscriptions quite that critically. In the case of South Arabia, it is more the various attempts to interpret evidence paleographically that confuse insight into and understanding of the Historical Period of South Arabia. De Maigret spoke of "the need for a totally new procedure, namely, the systematic archaeological exploration of southwestern Arabia, in order to gain a complete picture of Yemen's material culture and its development, and thus to approach the old question from a new perspective." Happily it can be said that this archaeological exploration has been intensified over the last two decades or so.

Relevant sources offer some examples from the Historical Period of South Arabia during the period from about 1000 to 500 B.C. First of all are the findings, albeit disputed, of the 1950-51 American excavation at Hajar bin Ḥumeid,[84] about 8 miles south of Timnaʿ. Pirenne[85] and J. Ryckmans[86] expressed some skepticism toward the conclusions drawn from the excavations, and I agree with Ryckmans that the two C-14 datings and the calculated mean value of 796 B.C. are not really convincing. More C-14 data are necessary in order to make a definitive dating. Nevertheless, these data and other results of the excavation cannot simply be ignored. Pottery from Hajar bin Ḥumeid, for example, especially the production methods ("burnished red slip technique"), have a lot in common with ceramics from the Syria-Palestine region; this is also the case regarding the type and method of painting. However, these ceramics are from the tenth-eighth century B.C., or at least the ninth-eighth.[87] The rather intensive discussions by Pirenne and J. Ryckmans did not even mention this early pottery. On the other hand, J. Zarins[88] was skeptical of this comparison, as made by Van Beek. The Zubayda site in central Arabia (Saudi Arabia) could become significant in this context. Several C-14 datings for this site led to a time span from 1300 to 635 B.C. Ceramics have been found from the earliest periods (1 and 2) that are similar to those from Hajar bin Ḥumeid. P. J. Parr and M. Gadar,[89] the excavators, thus felt it would be necessary to reexamine the pottery comparisons that Van Beek had conducted, this time including the Levant region. Finally, there is also the well-known monogrammed jar. Von Wissmann[90] dated this in the tenth-ninth century B.C., whereas Van Beek and W. F. Albright[91] suggested the ninth century B.C. as a probable dating. Von Wissmann and Van Beek assumed that the monogram was applied as a relief. In contrast, Ryckmans[92] considered it cursive and thus not comparable to the stonemason lettering of the inscription. However, he offered no dating.

In summary, it has been determined for Hajar bin Ḥumeid—on the basis of, above all, the pottery—that a dating around the ninth-eighth century B.C. is definitely plausible. Support for the order of layers suggested by Van Beek, and the resulting chronology—and thus the "Long Chronology"—has been provided by the American excavations at Wadi al-Jūbah,[93] halfway between Mārib and Timnaʿ. Here numerous C-14 data exist for the pre-Islamic period. The deepest layer at Hajar at-Tamrah yielded an uncalibrated C-14 dating of 1330 ± 110 B.C. (calibrated 1850-1385 B.C.) Other data also indicate that the site was abandoned around 400 B.C. at the latest. In any case, excavators believe that the various sites examined within Wadi al-Jūbah are from the ancient South Arabian civilization. They unanimously hold that here in Wadi al-Jūbah the "Long Chronology" has been confirmed.[94] In fact, they have suggested a beginning date of 1300 B.C.

Further archaeological "confirmation" that the Sabaean civilization started earlier than 500 B.C. has been provided by Alessandro de Maigret's[95] 1985 investigations in Wadi Yalā, a tributary of the major Wadi Dhana, at the mouth of which is the famous Mārib dam. De Maigret found a large settlement divided into three units: first, a "royal villa or residence"; second, about ten Sabaean workshops, then a small dam; and third, an outright city with a surrounding wall. Since all three complexes depended on use of the actual water management region, according to de Maigret, they might have been constructed at the same time. Archaeological and epigraphical data indicate a peak around the seventh-fifth centuries B.C. A ceramics comparison, however, shows it to be more probable that the entire complex goes all the way back to the tenth-ninth centuries B.C. It should be noted that according to G. Garbini, the epigraphist who analyzed the inscriptions, these inscriptions speak against the "Long Chronology."[96]

The French excavations in present-day Shabwa are also interesting, as probes there have revealed a series of fourteen layers.

According to C-14 data the oldest is from around 1550 B.C. (± 60, uncalibrated).[97]

Finally, the German Archaeological Institute has conducted geomorphological investigations in the Mārib oasis. According to these findings, the start of the irrigation period traces back to the late third millennium B.C. and the first permanent structures (A and B) were in operation by the first half of the first millennium B.C.[98] More recent investigations by W. Wagner[99] have even dated these sluice facilities to the middle or second half of the third millennium B.C.

These are some points that offer support for the "Long Chronology," though it is obvious that additional evidence in the form of archaeological finds is necessary to definitively confirm the "Long Chronology."

Some time ago, I heard about[100] a book *L'Arabie antique de Karib'īl à Mahomet. Nouvelles données sur l'histoire des Arabes grâce aux inscriptions.*[101] Editor and author of most of the articles was C. Robin, up to that time an advocate of Pirenne's "Short Chronology." Much to my surprise, Robin and J. Ryckmans, who also contributed an article to the volume, have now become supporters of the "Long Chronology." One of their main reasons are new excavation findings[102] with inscriptions, such as those at Yalā[103] (22 miles southwest of Mārib) and Raybūn[104] (in Wadi Ḥaḍramaut). In as-Sawdā', the ancient city of Nāshān in northern Yemen, a very archaic monumental inscription was found, repeated many times on columns. Due to the archaeological context, it was dated as coming from the eighth century B.C.[105] Furthermore, Robin dated the often-mentioned Karib'īl Watār a few generations prior to 535 B.C. and now considers it plausible that it might indeed be the Karibilu of the Assyrian inscription. And finally, he has shifted the beginning of the South Arabian civilization to the period between the thirteenth and tenth centuries B.C.[106] In the course of 1995, I heard of yet another book: *Documentation for Ancient Arabia,* by K. A. Kitchen. Kitchen too now views Pirenne's "Short Chronology" to be outdated, and has suggested that the "Old Sabaean Period" began around 1200 B.C.[107] With the death of Herrmann von Wissmann in 1979, an advocate of the "Long Chronology" unfortunately left the debate arena; also regrettable, the "main supporter" of the "Short Chronology," Jacqueline Pirenne, has since died as well, in 1990.

3. PRESENTATION OF THE KINGDOMS OF OLD SOUTH ARABIA

First and foremost the Sabaʾ kingdom must be named, with its capital[108] at Mārib. The chronological beginning of this kingdom, as apparent from the preceding discussion, is disputed among scholars in the field. I am in favor of setting the origins in the eighth century B.C. Even if the two Sabaeans mentioned in the Assyrian inscriptions, Yitaʿʾamar and Karibilu, are not the same persons as those named in the major Sabaic inscription (Gl 1703), there were in any case rulers in Sabaʾ in the eighth century B.C. Moreover, geomorphological investigations in the Mārib oasis have revealed[109] that the first permanently established irrigation structures already existed in the first half of the first millennium B.C.

The Sabaeans were long the ruling force in South Arabia. The beginning of the end of the independent kingdom of Sabaʾ was marked by the emergence of the Ḥimyarite kingdom at the end of the second century B.C. By around the middle of the second half of the third century A.D., Sabaʾ no longer played any significant role in political life. There was a Sabaeo-Ḥimyarite kingdom, but it was dominated by the Ḥimyarites.[110]

The next kingdom deserving mention is Maʿīn, the kingdom of the Minaeans. Its core territory was located in the al-Jauf river oasis, which begins northeast of Mārib. Opinions diverge with respect to the dates marking the beginning and end of this kingdom. Von Wissmann[111] named the period from about 420 to 120 B.C., similar to the dates given by W. W. Müller.[112] W. F. Albright[113] also set the commencement at around 400 or somewhat later, but he put the end within the timeframe of 50-25 B.C. Pirenne's[114] dating is from the fifth century B.C. to 200 A.D. J. Ryckmans[115] considered the starting date suggested by Albright to be too late, suggesting instead the middle of the sixth century B.C. as the beginning of the reign of the first

Minaean ruler. Ryckmans placed the end of the Minaean kingdom at 125 B.C. In its heyday, around the middle of the fourth century B.C., this state controlled a major segment of the incense route. Even in northern Arabia, in Dedān (now al-ʿUlā) in present-day Saudi Arabia, a Minaean colony existed to ensure the protection and security of the trade route. The worldwide connections of the Minaeans are apparent in the mention of Egypt and Gaza in Minaean texts. And on the Greek island of Delos, two Minaeans dedicated an altar to their local Moon God Wadd.[116]

Another kingdom that played an important role in early South Arabian history, as far as we know it, was the kingdom of ʾAusān. It was famous for its extensive trade relations, particularly with the eastern coast of Africa and extending as far as Zanzibar. Its center was in the highlands between Beiḥān, Wadi Markha, and the valleys of Niṣāb in the north and Audhilla and Dathina in the southeast.[117] Especially the Wusr region is often mentioned in the inscriptions. ʾAusān also had control of the coastal area, with Aden as the main port. The capital was Miswara in the interior of the country. Pirenne[118] believed to have rediscovered it, on the basis of comprehensive surveys, in the Wusr region at the site of the present-day town of Hajar as-Saʿada in Wadi Markha.

Our knowledge of the kingdom of ʾAusān is very limited and it is therefore difficult to determine precisely when it emerged.[119] We have only a date for when it came to an end, though this too is disputed. It is based on a victory inscription by the Sabaean mukarrib Karibʾīl Watār (RES 3945), according to which ʾAusān was utterly destroyed and its territory was ceded to Qatabān, still a Sabaean vassal at that time. Pirenne[120] dated this event as "around 460 B.C." and J. Ryckmans[121] "shortly before 400." Whereas von Wissmann originally[122] also supported a date at the end of the fifth century B.C., with reference to Ryckmans, in one of his last works[123] he gave the date as either 685 or 680 B.C. In addition, it cannot be ruled out that the kingdom of ʾAusān "reappeared" as a state at a later date, albeit reduced in size. This depends primarily on the dating of a statuette with an inscription, representing Yaṣduqʾil Farʿām Sharahʿat, an ʾAusān king. Von Wissmann and Höfner[124] referred to B. Schweitzer in dating it, based on the dress, as "during and before the mid-fifth century B.C." On the other hand, Pirenne[125] arrived at a dating in the first century A.D., as did C. Rathjens.[126] If the latter dating were correct, it would indeed indicate the "reappearance" of the kingdom of ʾAusān, though probably reduced in size.[127]

The Qatabānian kingdom was very significant; Wadi Beiḥān south of Sabaʾ was its central region. This is also where the capital city of Timnaʿ[128] (present-day Hajar Kuḥlān) was located. The chronological start of this kingdom is "of course" a subject of debate, depending on the dating of the previously mentioned report by the Sabaean ruler Karibʾīl Watār (RES 3945). This is where Qatabān was mentioned for the first time in an inscription. It was liberated from ʾAusān control but remained a Sabaean vassal. This event could have taken place between 685 and 430 B.C.[129] But Qatabān soon achieved its independence (400 B.C.[130]) and expended its territory considerably, now reaching as far as the Indian Ocean and to the al-Jūbah oasis to the north, almost a day's journey from Mārib.[131] For almost three centuries, Qatabān played an important role among the South Arabian kingdoms. Then two former districts of the Qatabānian kingdom, Ḥimyar and Radmān, were able to achieve their independence with the help of Sabaʾ, so that the state territory of Qatabān was reduced to a considerable extent. In particular, the coastal region was lost.[132] The ultimate defeat of Qatabān was achieved by Ḥaḍramaut, its neighbor to the east. There is also no agreement on when Timnaʿ was conquered and the kingdom came to an end. Albright[133] dated the event at 50 B.C.; von Wissmann[134] 100 A.D.; and Pirenne[135] set the destruction of Timnaʿ at around 200 A.D. and the end of the kingdom at around 250 A.D.

The kingdom of Ḥaḍramaut far to the east must also be mentioned here. Today the name essentially refers only to the steep wadi about 125 miles in length running parallel to the South Arabian coast at a distance of about 100 miles. In antiquity, however, this kingdom comprised an area including the frankincense region of Dhofār to the east, in present-day Oman, and extending to the shores of the Indian Ocean in the south. In the north it bordered on the great sandy desert, Rubʿ al-Khālī. Shabwat, the capital (present-day Shabwa), was locat-

Zafār: castle ruin

ed at the westernmost tip of the kingdom, at the edge of the Ramlat Ṣayhad desert. This location is understandable since it was along the incense route. Initially, the Ḥaḍramaut kingdom was a vassal of Sabaʾ, but it was able to gain independence in the fourth century B.C. By having possession of the Dhofār, the actual frankincense cultivation region, and the important harbors of Qanaʾ and Sumhuram (in Oman), for a certain period of time Ḥaḍramaut was one of the most important and powerful states in South Arabia. Since the Ḥaḍramitic inscriptions are not very significant in terms of either number or length, it is difficult to reconstruct the history of this kingdom. It is necessary to refer to, above all, Sabaic inscriptions and Greek and Roman sources. The decline of the kingdom of Ḥaḍramaut is, again, difficult to date definitively. Müller[136] and Brian Doe[137] mentioned the second decade of the fourth century A.D. and the mid-fourth century, respectively, whereas J.-F. Breton[138] and von Wissmann–M. Höfner[139] have attributed the defeat of the Ḥaḍramaut to the Sabaeo-Ḥimyarite ruler Shammar Yuharʿish, who reigned alone starting in 295 A.D.

The last kingdom to appear chronologically, though by no means was it insignificant, is the Ḥimyar kingdom. The Ḥimyarites appear to have originally been vassals of the Qatabānian kingdom, as their central territory was located in a formerly Qatabānian region.[140] The capital was Ẓafār (in the former North Yemen, east of the Yarim-Ibb road). The Ḥimyar period began in 115 B.C.,[141] but it was not documented in inscriptions until the first century A.D. The exact reason for this date remains unclear; perhaps it was the date of their independence.[142] The subsequent centuries were definitely marked by conflicts between Ḥimyar and Sabaʾ, and in the end the Ḥimyarites emerged victorious (approximately the middle of the second half of the third century[143]). Their final adversary was Ḥaḍramaut, which was defeated between roughly 300 and 350 A.D.[144] In 523 the Abyssinians conquered the land and at the end of the sixth century Yemen temporarily became a Sasanid province, to become Muslim a short time later.

4. THE HISTORY OF SOUTH ARABIA FROM THE TENTH CENTURY B.C. TO THE SEVENTH CENTURY A.D.

Based on the preceding discussion, the problems associated with offering a detailed presentation of the history of the ancient South Arabian kingdoms have certainly been made clear. Until further archaeological expeditions are conducted and new inscriptions are found, gaps will remain in the knowledge of the history of ancient South Arabia.

Readers of this small book might ask why this chapter begins with the tenth century B.C., though I have previously said that I view Sabaean history as having begun in the eighth century B.C. The explanation is relatively clear. This makes it possible to discuss at least briefly the famous story of the Queen of Sheba's visit with Solomon. It can clearly be shown that Grohmann[145] was incorrect in suggesting that the names Sabaʾ and Sabum in Sumerian texts from the third century B.C. refer to the Sabaeans; however, it is not all that clear whether the Queen of Sheba (Sabaʾ)'s visit with King Solomon as described in 1 Kings 10 actually took place or not. I think Pirenne[146] oversimplified the issue by ironically asking advocates of the "Long Chronology" whether this was rooted in the end in the "sweet desire to place the Queen of Sheba, who must have lived in the tenth century B.C., into the chronological order." Von Wissmann[147] was convinced that this visit did in fact take place. It is further undisputed that there were queens in Arabia, as is clear from the Assyrian annals. Only the names Zabība, Shamshi, and Teʾelhunu are named, all of whom lived during the eighth century B.C.[148] Even if we do not know the name of the legendary "Queen of Sheba," we can nonetheless agree with Müller[149] when he wrote the following about the report in the *Book of Kings:* "It is a report, the historical core of which probably lies in the expansion of trade relations." It should not be overlooked, however, that the report in the *Book of Kings* did not assume its final form until the sixth century, that is, four hundred years later.

Incidentally, the distance from Mārib to Jerusalem was about 1500 miles. Assuming the distance that could be covered in a day by a pack camel to be under 20 miles, the Queen of Sheba would have been on the road for about 160 days, or over five months, for the round trip. Since a segment of this journey was outside Sabaean territory it can be assumed that agreements had been made with the ruling tribes there in order to ensure safe passage and provisions for the caravans.[150]

An Assyrian clay tablet inscription published in 1990[151] that had been found at excavations in the environs of Haditha (roughly 150 miles northwest of Baghdad) reports that a governor of Suchu and Mari (mid-Euphrates) who reigned around the mid-eighth century B.C. raided a caravan from Teima and Saba' near the city of Ḫindanu (near present-day Abu Kemal). Aside from Biblical passages, this is the oldest extant inscription that mentions Saba'. In a relatively recent essay[152] M. Liverani has written that the small Ḫindanu kingdom was the only one in the region that paid tribute to Assyria with dromedaries, as well as with myrrh, purple-died textiles, and alabaster. This was documented in the annals of the Assyrian king Tukulti-Ninurta (890-884 B.C.). On the other hand, at the time of Tiglath Pileser I (1114-1026 B.C.), Ḫindanu was neither independent nor had it begun its later practice of paying tribute with exotic goods. Liverani thus assumed that Ḫindanu had served as a caravan base between South Arabia and Mesopotamia between 1075 and 890 B.C. The start of trade relations with South Arabia in the second half of the tenth century B.C. would definitely fit in with the Queen of Sheba's visit with Solomon (approx. 960-920 B.C.).

In this context, it is helpful to determine when the Sabaeans first settled in the Mārib area. It is assumed that at the time of Solomon's reign they still lived in the Dedān region (Saudi Arabia), that is, in North Arabia, later migrating to South Arabia.[153] J. Ryckmans,[154] however, has suggested that the Sabaeans originally inhabited southwestern Yemen and later moved to Mārib. Von Wissmann[155] too found this migration plausible. In contrast to Ryckmans, who at the time supported the "Short Chronology," von Wissmann emphasized that such a migration took place "some time before the tenth century B.C."

Ṣirwāḥ appears to have been the initial capital of the Sabaean kingdom, the center later moving to Mārib.

Recent excavation findings of the Americans in Wadi al-Jūbah and, especially, those of de Maigret in the Wadi Dhana area confirm uninterrupted inhabitation there since at least the tenth century B.C. This tends to suggest von Wissmann's earlier date. In my view, Sabaean civilization cannot simply have appeared in the limelight of history in the fifth century B.C. with an alphabet and architectural wonders as well as a completed system of irrigation. Additional archaeological investigations are needed to fill in the present gaps in our knowledge. Presently it can be said that Sabaeans have been documented in Assyrian inscriptions from the end of the eighth century B.C. or, to be more precise, in 715 and again in 685 B.C.[156] One of the first Sabaean inscriptions is the previously discussed report by Karib'īl Watār (RES 3945) on the military campaign against ʾAusān, though there are a number of datings for it, ranging from 685 to 400 B.C. To aid comprehension, this inscription is cited in part below:

> . . . and he (Karib'īl) beat it [i.e., ʾAusān] in Wusr [the capital; stands for ʾAusān], until he swept away ʾAusān and its king Murattaʿum; and the elders of the council of ʾAusān designated it [ʾAusān] for Samahat [possibly the main goddess of ʾAusān], but he [Karib'īl] designated it for death and imprisonment; and (when) he called for the destruction of his [i.e., the ʾAusānite king's] palace, Maswar [the name of the royal palace], and the removal of all inscriptions mentioning Karib'īl from his palace [Maswar] and the inscriptions from the temples of his gods and he . . . led back his palace Maswar and the children of ʾAlmaqah [stands for the Sabaeans] and the tribal confederation, his freemen and his slaves, from the territories of ʾAusān and its cities. . . .[157]

This war started because of the activities of the ruler of ʾAusān, which was itself a Sabaean vassal, against Ḥaḍramaut, another Sabaean vassal.

The seventh and sixth centuries B.C. can be seen as the zenith of the Sabaean kingdom's power. The same inscription also reports of the expansion of the kingdom's territory to the northwest in the area of Najrān. During this time—von Wissmann[158] and others[159] gave an even earlier date, namely, the tenth century B.C.—the Sabaeans also expanded their rule toward Ethiopia, that is, on the opposite side of the Red Sea. Pirenne,[160] on the other hand, dated this in the fifth century B.C. South Arabian influence was noticeable there primarily in the writing, religion, and language.

Yadaᶜʾil Dhārih, a successor to Karibʾīl Watār, then erected three temples to honor ʾAlmaqah (Ilumqah) the moon god and chief deity of the kingdom, two of which continue to impress visitors even today: Maḥram Bilqis/ʾAwwām near Mārib and the large round temple in Ṣirwāḥ. The third structure is located near al-Masājid, 18 miles south of Mārib. Unfortunately it has not been well preserved. Somewhat later—the second half of the sixth century B.C.[161]—the great dam of Mārib was built. Inscriptions (CIH 622, 623)[162] indicate that two successive rulers worked on this "wonder of the world."

The political situation at this time—seventh-sixth centuries B.C.—was approximately as follows: The Sabaʾ tribe had its center at Mārib and Ṣirwāḥ. It's main territory was relatively small, but it was extended considerably through the vassal states under Sabaean control. Two types of vassals need to be distinguished here. One was totally dependent, directly under Sabaean rule, and the other involved a protective dominance that Sabaʾ exerted over a tribe. The tribe itself retained a certain degree of independence, but was still obliged to pay tribute to Sabaʾ. Both vassal types were required to honor the chief Sabaean deity ʾAlmaqah.[163] The leader of Sabaʾ and its vassal states was the mukarrib, the "unifier of the land."[164]

The status of the other kingdoms that later gained power and independence, such as Maᶜīn, Qatabān, and Ḥaḍramaut, is somewhat unclear for this time period. In Robin's[165] view, the last two kingdoms named were allies ("brothers") of Sabaʾ, since Karibʾīl mentioned the names of their state deities.

The first mention of the Minaeans was in an inscription (RES 3943)[166] by Yiṯaᶜʾamar Bayyin, the second ruler involved in the building of the Mārib dam. Therein, Maᶜīn was defeated along with

Muhaʾmir (Najrān, Saudi Arabia) and Amir (region between Najrān and Maʿīn). At this time, the mid- to late fifth century B.C., the kingdom of ʾAusān was also clearly defeated in several campaigns led by the Sabaeans.[167]

It can be assumed that Sabaʾ's "rival kingdoms," that is, Maʿīn, Qatabān, and Ḥaḍramaut, had already experienced a period of independence before they became vassals of Sabaʾ and then, ultimately, independent states. Von Wissmann[168] came to this conclusion on the basis of the difference of these three languages or dialects as compared to Sabaic.

In any case, these three kingdoms probably gained their independence from Sabaʾ starting around 400 B.C.[169] It is known from an inscription (RES 3858) that Sabaʾ suffered a terrible defeat against Qatabān around 370,[170] losing parts of its territory in the south.

The earliest Minaean royal inscription (RES 2980) is from Yaṯill (present-day Barāqish) and dated at around 420 B.C.[171] Inscriptions from a short time later are also extant from the capital Qarnāwu. The Minaeans apparently gained their independence from Sabaʾ with the help of the Ḥaḍramaut kingdom.[172] By the mid-fourth century B.C. at the latest,[173] they had replaced the Sabaeans as rulers of the incense route, which they then controlled together with Ḥaḍramaut.

From this point on, four kingdoms coexisted: Sabaʾ, Maʿīn, Qatabān, and Ḥaḍramaut. But the balance of power that more or less existed was not to last forever.

Between 125 and 120 B.C. the situation began to change, events apparently having been triggered by the Ḥimyar tribe. This raises new questions. Who exactly were the Ḥimyarites? We encounter their name for the first time in a Ḥaḍramitic inscription (RES 2687) from the early first century A.D.,[174] which reports of the construction of the wall of Qalat (north of the Ḥaḍramitic port of Qanaʾ, near Biʾr ʿAlī). Also, Pliny (Nat. Hist. book VI, xxxii, 161) mentioned that the Homerites, the Ḥimyarites, were the greatest in number.[175]

The Ḥimyarites represent a problem to the extent that they are viewed as a single tribe by most scholars.[176] Beeston,[177] on the other hand, distinguished between the "lesser" and the "greater" Ḥimyarites. The former, according to Beeston, lived at the Indian Ocean coast around Wadi Mayfaʿa, and the Ḥaḍramites supposedly built the wall of Qalat as protection against this group. The latter were settled almost 200 miles further west in Wadi Banah. Von Wissmann assumed that the homeland of the Ḥimyarites was the present-day highlands of Yafaʿ, northwest of Aden. This region belonged to the Qatabān kingdom and was called Dahas until the Ḥimyarites achieved independence. However, elsewhere[178] von Wissmann wrote that the Ḥimyarites originally settled further to the east and migrated westward, this migration having led to the wars starting in 120 B.C.

The Ḥimyarites definitely conquered parts of Qatabān, and the Ḥimyaritic era began in 115 B.C. This year marks the beginning of Ḥimyar as an independent state.[179] The capital of the kingdom was at Ẓafār, in the mountains south of Yarim, at an altitude of almost 10,000 feet.

A lengthy period followed during which everyone was at war with everyone else, whereby the coalitions changed frequently. As mentioned elsewhere,[180] the dates when individual kingdoms came to an end are widely disputed among scholars. One can say with certainty at least that the kingdoms of Maʿīn and Qatabān were the first to go. The "victors" of the conflicts were ultimately Sabaʾ, Ḥimyar, and Ḥaḍramaut. The altercations between Sabaʾ and Ḥimyar are interesting, yet also lacking agreement among researchers. There is often mention of a Sabaeo-Ḥimyar kingdom, as if there were a single, united state, but this was not the case. The rulers of the respective kingdoms often claimed possession of the other and they often waged war against each other. The rulers of the two kingdoms often used the same title: "King of Sabaʾ and Dhū-Raydān," in which Dhū-Raydān referred to the fortress at the Ḥimyaritic capital of Ẓafār.[181]

Even after the disappearance of the kingdom of Maʿīn, Sabaʾ was unable to succeed the Minaean kingdom along its section of the incense route. After the Minaean colony was disbanded in Dedān, the Nabataeans appeared on the scene. They established a trade station in al-Ḥijr (present-day Madain Salih, Saudi Arabia), north of Dedān. Since the Nabataeans and the Sabaeans soon became enemies, the incense route began to lose significance.

Around this time a non-Arabian power appeared in South Arabia to at least try to alter the power situation there in its favor once and for all. It was the Romans.[182] At the outset, Augustus had annexed the once-so-powerful Egypt into the Roman empire in 30 B.C. Rome thus controlled the Egyptian Red Sea ports. Since the overland route to India and China, the famous "Silk Road," was always dependent on relations with the Parthians—which were often sufficiently poor—it was natural for the Romans to turn their interest toward the sea route to India. Here they faced two obstacles, the Sabaeans and the Ḥimyarites. The former had the "Bab al-Mandab," the "gateway of tears," South Arabia's westernmost point. And the latter held Aden. Moreover, both kingdoms were friendly toward the Parthian kingdom. Thus Rome had to secure a sea route. The way to "pacify" Saba' and Ḥimyar was virtually prescribed, via the "incense route." An attack from the Red Sea shore would have been much more difficult because of the mountains and the fact that Mārib—the capital of Saba'—was at the edge of the desert.

So Augustus dispatched a large army under the leadership of Aelius Gallus, prefect in Egypt, in the summer of 25 B.C. In addition to the Roman contingent, this army also included 1000 Nabataean camel-riders and 500 Jewish archers. Syllaios, a Nabataean, who as chancellor carried on the government affairs of the still-dependent Nabataean king, Obodas III, was an advisor in this campaign. Strabo,[183] reporting on this military action, described it in the darkest of colors, yet it cannot be said with certainty whether Syllaios was responsible for its failure or not. It is nevertheless clear that it was definitely not in the interest of the Nabataeans for Rome to gain control of the incense route.

The campaign began with the conquering of Najrān, the border city separating the Nabataean and Sabaean kingdoms. Soon the old Minaean city of Yaṯill surrendered without a struggle and the Roman army continued on toward Mārib. The city was besieged for six days and then the aggressors retreated, probably for reasons of sickness and/or lack of water. After nine days they reached Najrān and a short time later, the territory of the former Nabataean kingdom. Although this might sound like very few days, it is assumed that the campaign in Arabia, from Leuke Kome to Mārib and back, as far as Hygrā, lasted from June (or July) 25 B.C. until about February 24 B.C.[184]

The Christian era brought a regrouping of the states that still existed in South Arabia. First of all, the remainder of Qatabān was eliminated by Ḥaḍramaut. As previously mentioned, there is disagreement as to exactly when this occurred.[185] The vast majority date it within the range 100 to 200 A.D. Saba᾽ itself is supposed to have been threatened when Ḥimyar allied with Ḥaḍramaut against the Sabaeans. These struggles must have started shortly after the start of the Christian era,[186] leading to Ḥimyar's taking of parts of the Sabaean territory. During this time, the Ḥimyarites established their capital with the fortress Raydān in the highlands at Ẓafār, which Pliny referred to as Sapphar.[187]

As previously mentioned, the rulers of Saba᾽ and Ḥimyar carried the same title, "King of Saba᾽ and Dhū-Raydān," thus clearly staking their respective claims to the territories of their adversary. Furthermore, the Sabaean kingdom broke down into separate dynasties, or clans. First there was the traditional dynasty at Mārib, and there were four additional dynasties in the highlands: the Hamdān at Nāʿiṭ (almost 60 miles north of Sanaa, near Raida), the Banū Bataʿ at Ḥāz (almost 20 miles northwest of Sanaa, near Shibam), Martadum of Shibam Aqyān (a little over 20 miles northwest of Sanaa and ʿAmrān, present-day Shibam), and finally Gurat at the foot of the Jabal Yislah pass).[188] These different highland dynasties often fought bitter wars against each other, sometimes allying with other South Arabian kingdoms.

Robin[189] views the beginning of the Christian era as marking the start of the second period in the history of South Arabia. The first segment, according to Robin, started in the seventh century B.C. and ended with the close of the first century A.D. This was the period of the "royal caravan leaders." It was dominated by the tribes settled at the periphery of the desert and its main activities were connected to the incense trade.

The second period, starting with the first century A.D., on the other hand, was dominated by the highland tribes. In the north around Sanaa there were various Sabaean tribes; in the south, the Ḥimyarites, with their capital at Ẓafār, who predominated during this segment of South Arabian history. It should also be mentioned that Sabaʾ was also threatened by Arab bedouins.[190] In the course of the second century A.D. the traditional dynasty at Mārib played their last card, and from the last quarter of the second century it was now ʿAlhān Nahfān of the Hamdān dynasty who reigned over the Sabaean kingdom. But Mārib retained its significance as a religious center.[191]

ʿAlhān Nahfān allied himself with Gadūrat, king of the Abyssinians, who controlled the Tihāma at the Red Sea (around 200).[192] His son Shaʿirum Awtar, on the other hand, fought against the Abyssinians. He succeeded in fact, in 217-218, in defeating the Ḥaḍramitic army at the battle of Shuwaʾrān, taking their king prisoner. In the aftermath, Shabwa was plundered. Another campaign brought him to Central Arabia to the Kinda kingdom, whose capital was at Qaryat Ḏāt Kāhilim (present-day Qaryat al-Fāw, Saudi Arabia, about 175 miles northeast of Najrān).

The Hamdānids soon had to relinquish their power to the Gurat dynasty, since we know from inscriptions that two of their rulers, ʾIlsharaḥ Yaḥḍib and Yaʾzil Bayyin, reigned over Sabaʾ together and even managed to conquer Ḥimyar in a battle around 248-49. There is relatively good information available on this segment of South Arabian history due to, above all, the inscriptions found by the American expedition at Mārib[193] and the expedition at Miʿsāl[194] (about 90 miles southeast of Sanaa, halfway between Radāʿ and al-Bayḍā).

By the middle of the second half of the third century[195] there were only two kingdoms still in existence: the Sabaeo-Ḥimyar—whereby the Ḥimyarites most likely set the tone and between around 270 and 280 they ultimately defeated Sabaʾ[196]—and the Ḥaḍramaut kingdoms. In the late third century[197] Shammar Yuharʿish, the Ḥimyar ruler, then defeated Ḥaḍramaut. From this point on, the Ḥimyar kings carried the title "King of Sabaʾ and Dhū-Raydān and Ḥaḍramaut and Yamanat." The precise meaning of the word Yamanat is not known. Perhaps it denoted the region that used to belong to ʾAusān and Qatabān,[198] or else the coastal region south of Ḥaḍramaut.[199] Shabwa, the famous capital of Ḥaḍramaut, was destroyed and vanished from history. Shibam became the new capital, in the middle of Wadi Ḥaḍramaut. In von Wissmann's opinion, the Sabaeo-Ḥimyar ruler himself chose this

Shibam, South Yemen

site and forced a majority of the population of Shabwa to resettle there.[200] Von Wissmann also indicated that the destruction and desolation of the great Shabwa oasis was certainly not without consequences. With that, an important part of the settled region of South Arabia was transformed into desert. While the distance between the Mārib and Shabwa oases had previously been less than 90 miles, there was now a huge gap ovber 480 miles between Ḥaḍramaut and the rest of Yemen. This gap encouraged migrations to the region as well as belligerent invasions.

The "international" significance of the Sabaeo-Ḥimyar kingdom is apparent in the fact that the Ḥimyar ruler Shammar Yuharʿish dispatched his governor in Sabaʾ as an ambassador to the court of the Sasanids in Seleucia-Ctesiphon. According to Müller this occurred prior to 297.[201]

In the early fourth century, Ḥaḍramaut was able to liberate itself again for a short time from Sabaeo-Ḥimyar domination, but it was reconquered once and for all in the second decade of the fourth century.[202]

An inscription from the second half of the fourth century (Ja 671) reports of the first break in the Mārib dam.[203] The end of polytheism in the Sabaeo-Ḥimyar kingdom also came around this time. The chief deity ʾAlmaqah (Ilumqah) and the others were replaced by Raḥmānān, "the merciful," who was referred to as "ruler of the heavens." Whether this form of monotheism was Christian or Jewish is unclear.[204] The last known inscriptions in the ʾAwwām temple in Mārib that were dedicated to ʾAlmaqah are also from this period. The break in the dam had already represented a great blow to the inhabitants of the Mārib oasis, but soon after the entire Sabaeo-Ḥimyar kingdom was to suffer another major setback. The former Sabaean colony of Abyssinia had since become a powerful kingdom in its own right, from which emerged the kingdom of Aksum at the beginning of the Christian era, named after the capital city of Aksum in the mountainous region of northern Abyssinia. Several German expeditions have contributed to the exploration of this region. The first king about whom precise information is available was ʿĒzānā, who converted to Christianity. This ruler probably reigned during the first half of the fourth century.[205] His title mentions Ḥimyar and Dhū-Raydān, Saba᾽ and Salḥin (Royal Palace at Mārib), as well as the Tihāma. Ḥaḍramaut and Yamanat, on the other hand, are not mentioned. It is definitely plausible that this means that ʿĒzānā had conquered a large part of South Arabia, and only the eastern regions of Ḥaḍramaut and Yamanat were still independent, though this has not been documented in inscriptions.

Around the mid-fourth century[206] the Roman emperor Constantine II (337-361) dispatched a delegation under Theophilos, an arianistic bishop, to Ẓafār to convert the Ḥimyar ruler, whose name is not known,[207] to Christianity. This ruler ordered that Christian churches be erected at his expense at Ẓafār, Aden, and further east in a city not referred to by name—probably Hormuz[208]—on the Persian Gulf.

Under Abākarib Asʿad, who reigned in the first third of the fifth century,[209] the Sabaeo-Ḥimyar kingdom experienced another peak. To to day Arabian tradition considers him the greatest ruler in ancient South Arabia.[210] He was able to extend the kingdom as far as Central Arabia, and it is said that he came as far as Yaṯrib (Medīna), where he was converted to Judaism. Even if inscriptions show that there were many Jews, also surrounding the king, there is no definite evidence of this.[211] The king's title was "King of Saba᾽ and Dhū-Raydān and Ḥaḍramaut and Yamanat and their (pluralis majestatis) Arabs in the highlands and lowlands (Tihāma)." Von Wissmann[212] has suggested that the Arabs in the highlands and lowlands probably referred to the bedouins in Central Arabia and along the coastal region of Hejaz, since the South Arabians did not refer to themselves as Arabs.[213] These would mean an official acknowledgment of the Arab-bedouin element. The bedouins had become neighbors to the peasant population of the large Sabaeo-Ḥimyar state in an extended circle around the Ṣayhad and the Rubʿ al-Khālī deserts in the east and north.[214] Robin[215] spoke of an "Etat binational," a mixture of the large number of Arab tribes with the traditional South Arabian tribes.

An early sign of the decline of the ancient South Arabian civilization was the next break in the Mārib dam in 450.[216] An inscription tells us that a year earlier, large sections of the dam had already had to be repaired and, when parts of the dam were destroyed in 450,

20,000 men were put to work to repair it. These events fell during the reign of Shuraḥbiʾil Yaʿfur, son of the great Abūkarib Asʿad. As documented by an inscription, he had a large palace built at Ẓafār.

Arab-Islamic tradition tells of a ruler named Abdkulal who reigned in the period following. He is supposed to have converted to Christianity, but this is not documented in inscriptions.[217]

There is also an Ethiopian source from the second half of the fifth century, the so-called martyrs accounts of Azqir, which provide evidence that there was a large Christian community in Najrān.[218]

The sixth century is rather well documented by a number of inscriptions. We know that in 516, King Maʿdikarib Yaʿfur undertook a military campaign to Central Arabia to battle the rebel bedouins. Shortly after assuming the throne, Yūsuf Asʾar Yaṭʿar (Dhū-Nuwās of Arab tradition), the Jewish "King of all Tribes,"[219] began warring against the Abyssinians within the country and against Christians in general.[220] According to Müller, the motive behind the persecution was not purely religious in nature, but to a large extent political. Much of the local population considered the South Arabian kings at this time to be puppets of the court of Aksum. It must be taken into account that as early as the beginning of the sixth century the Christian bishop Thomas had asked Abyssinian troops to enter the country to protect the Christians, thus limiting the sovereignty of the local ruler.[221] The local ruler had to heed this mood in the country, which wanted to limit the influence of the Byzantine empire at the Red Sea, since Byzantium supported the kingdom of Aksum.

The persecution began by conquering Ẓafār and killing all Abyssinians living there. Churches and fortresses in the country were destroyed and the coastal plateau was recaptured. In 518 or 523,[222] after a long siege, Najrān was taken and its Christian inhabitants killed. Retaliation by the Abyssinians did not come until 525. The Abyssinian King Ella Aṣbaḥā, who had the biblical name Kālēb, led the operation himself, whereby he could count on Byzantine support, especially on the water.[223] The local army was defeated, Yūsuf was killed, and Yemen became an Abyssinian protectorate. Kālēb eternalized himself with victory inscriptions in Mārib and Ẓafār, had churches built, and chose a local nobleman of the Yazʿanid dynasty to reign as a vassal king; the chosen nobleman, Ṣimyafaʿ Ashwaʿ, converted from Judaism to Christianity in order to take the throne. In 530-31[224] a man named Abrehā, who had served in the Aksumite army, staged a revolt and took power. He had belonged to the Aksumite troops that had remained in Yemen even after Kālēb's victory and his retreat to Aksum. Kālēb attempted, in two futile campaigns, to regain power. According to Müller,[225] Abrehā was still serving as Kālēb's viceroy or governor in 542. Inscriptions do not refer to him as king until 547. Shortly before 542[226] the Mārib dam broke yet again and required the services of many workers and considerable material expenses for the repairs.

The last extant Ḥimyaritic inscription (CIH 325) is from 554. The succeeding decades showed signs of the unstoppable decline of ancient South Arabia. The bedouin element was becoming more and more noticeable. The Kinda dynasty was apparently forced out of Central Arabia and moved back to their original homeland, Ḥaḍramaut. It is unclear exactly when this resettlement took place. Von Wissmann[227] has suggested the first half of the sixth century, and Robin[228] the seventh. The "gap" that emerged through the destruction of Shabwa and the disappearance of the Ḥaḍramaut kingdom was certainly favorable for the invasion of the Kindas.

As far as we know, Abrehā led two other campaigns. First, he attacked the Maʿadd tribe in Central Arabia in 547, as is confirmed in inscriptions. The second military campaign was much more spectacular. It took place around 570 or a little earlier,[229] in other words at the end of the reign of Abrehā, and was against Mecca, though they never got that far. The undertaking was so "spectacular" for the Arabs because Abrehā had an elephant[230] within his army, which is why the Koran mentions the "people of the elephant." The "elephant year," 570, was of course "even more significant" since according to Islamic tradition it was the year of Muhammad's birth.

Relatively speaking, there is a lot of information on the religious situation at the time of Abrehā and on his personal religious convictions. Later, Christianity again gained considerable ground. At first Monophysitism predominated, which was also widespread in Abyssinia. After that, the Chalcedonian form[231] prevalent in the

Byzantine empire gained the upper hand. Müller[232] has suggested that two church hierarchies might have existed in South Arabia under Abrehā, namely, a Chalcedonian one in Ẓafār and one of the opponents of Chalcedon in Najrān. Among other things, Abrehā had a large cathedral erected in Sanaa.

When Abrehā died around 570, he was succeeded by Sayf ibn Dhī Yazan. Sometime between 575 and 580,[233] the dam must have broken yet again. This time it brought the end of this "wonder of the world." The event was recorded in the Koran (sura 34:15-17), where there is a report on the desolation of the Mārib oases. A large part of the population emigrated. Research offers various explanations for this migration, including reduced precipitation, economic motives, and changes in political relations to the effect that the major power centers had shifted to the highlands and Mārib continued to lose importance.[234] In my view, several of the reasons mentioned contributed to the emigration. Between 570 and 575[235] groups in South Arabia that were friendly toward the Persians went to the Persian Sasanids to request help in opposing the Abyssinians. They did receive support but perhaps not in the way they imagined. The Abyssinians were indeed chased out by the Sasanids, who were supported by the local population. But after that, South Arabia was made a Persian vassal state and, in 597-98, it was run by a Persian governor as a province of the Sasanid empire.

Muhammad conquered Mecca in 630. A short time earlier, in 628, the Sasanids had suffered a serious defeat in battle against Byzantium. Their great king Chosroes II was then murdered. The Persian satrap in Yemen—the fifth Persian governor named Bādhān—converted to Islam. It is not known whether the inhabitants of South Arabia also converted, but it can be assumed that only few did so.[236]

The local population probably viewed relations to Medīna more from a political perspective.[237] It was thus fitting that al-Muhājir Abū Umayya ibn al-Mughīra, Medīna's representative in Sanaa, was a financial advisor. The most important issue seemed to be the levying of poor and property taxes. The Yemenite nobility was not content with the new situation. A counter-prophet, al-Aswad alʿAnsī, led a revolt in 632. The rebels opposing al-Muhājir and his followers—

who were supported by the descendants of the Persian soldiers, the "Abnā"—experienced temporary victory, but were defeated in the end. Medīna retained control and al-Muhājir became the first governor of the al-Yaman province in the Islamic empire.

5. CONCLUSION

If one attempts to sum up the ancient South Arabian civilization, it should first of all be noted that, as far as historically comprehensible, the civilization lasted for at least 1400 years (from roughly 800 B.C. to 600 A.D.). Its "longevity" surpassed all other ancient Middle Eastern kingdoms. The individual kingdoms that emerged from this civilization, however, did not last as long, with the possible exception of the Sabaeans. The end of the ancient South Arabian civilization marked the dawn of a new epoch—a new age and calendar—in this part of the Middle East, and ancient Middle Eastern history in general also came to an end. Nevertheless, ruins and inscriptions in present-day Yemen continue to recall the glorious past of South Arabia. The best example of this is the new dam at Mārib, not far from the original structure. When it was opened in 1986, a stela was erected emphasizing the historical continuity between the two structures. The text is written in both Arabic and Sabaic. Robin[238] has also noted that the Old South Arabic language can be found on the diplomas issued by the University in Sanaa and on cigarette packages.

The 1400 years of Old South Arabia without a doubt mark one of the high points in ancient Middle Eastern culture and civilization as a whole. One needs only to think of the architecture, which made use, above all, of stone as a building material, replacing the brick that had been used almost exclusively up to that time. Prime examples documenting this are the temples, city walls, and last but not least the irrigation systems, especially in Mārib, which were unique in the entire ancient Middle East. Finally, the magnificently organized system of trade along the famous incense route was another remarkable achievement.

Considering the fact that, in comparison with other fields, the archaeological exploration of the Middle East of antiquity is still in its beginnings, then a lot of pleasant surprises surely await us that will add to the already great impression observers have received of ancient South Arabian civilization.

Inevitably a question must be raised that poses itself again and again, for other cultures as well: Why did this civilization come to an end? What caused the decline? Clearly there were many contributing factors. The emergence of Islam and the incorporation of Yemen into the Islamic empire surely marked the chronological end point, but this event was not really definitive by that time. The decline of Old South Arabia had begun much earlier.

In my view, Aksum's taking of southern Yemen around 525 A.D. marked the chronological beginning of the end. After that, other events and reasons contributed to its ultimate destruction. Of course it cannot be forgotten that there were also events prior to 525 that by no means added to South Arabia's strength: for example, the wars the individual kingdoms fought against each other and the decline in overland transport of incense in favor of the sea route once the rhythm of the monsoon winds were understood.[239] Even possible climatic changes cannot be ruled out.[240] Finally, penetration by bedouin tribes starting around the third century A.D. and thus the "Arabization" of the region was certainly an added reason for the decline.[241] By then the destruction of Mārib when the dam broke represented merely a symbolic closing act.

VI. Social Structures in Ancient South Arabia

The following is an attempt to offer an overview of the social structures in the region, based on extant archaeological finds and inscriptions. In doing this, I think it is necessary to distinguish at least two phases or developments. The first deals with the situation at the time roughly before the eighth century B.C., that is, a large part of the second millennium B.C. or the Bronze Age. The second phase would then be the "Mukarrib Period" starting at around the eighth century B.C., as this title starts to appear in inscriptions around this time. Some researchers, however, such as K. A. Kitchen,[1] regard this period as beginning as early as around 1200 B.C. Robin[2] is somewhat more cautious, setting the beginning of the "South Arabian civilization" at somewhere between the thirteenth and tenth centuries B.C. He did not speak of mukarribs when referring to this period. Since most proponents of the "Long Chronology" do not date the oldest inscriptions any earlier than the eighth century B.C., it can be said that the title "mukarrib" has not been documented in inscriptions until this time. Of course this does not rule out the possibility that there were mukarribs even earlier, but as yet no evidence of this has been found.

It is a matter of opinion whether or not it is useful to distinguish additional periods. The replacement of the title "mukarrib" by "king" (malik) could be seen as a further division. But when did this occur? According to von Wissmann[3] it was around 525 B.C. and according to Robin[4] the expression "mukarrib" fell out of use in Sabaʾ starting in the third century B.C., though it did appear in Qatabān and later in Ḥaḍramaut. Furthermore, some rulers carried both titles.[5]

As already mentioned, Robin[6] used different criteria to identify periods. From the eighth to the end of the first century B.C the royal caravan leaders set the tone. They belonged to the tribes at the peripheries of the desert and their most important activity was the incense trade. Robin defined the second period as extending from the first to the sixth centuries A.D. during which the tribes of the highlands ("hautes terres") were more significant. This included the tribes around Sanaa and the commonwealth of tribes of Dhū-Raydān or Ḥimyar, with Ẓafār as its capital. This division seems more sound and comprehensible from a historical perspective than periods determined on the basis of mukarribs and kings. Nonetheless, I would set the beginning of the latter period much earlier, at the end of the second century B.C., to mark the beginning of the Ḥimyar dynasty around 115 B.C. A decisive shift of power took place at that time.[7] The Maʿīn kingdom, as well as parts of Qatabān, were conquered by Sabaʾ. Moreover, the commonwealth of Dhū-Raydān or the Ḥimyarites achieved independence within Qatabān.

1. THE BRONZE AGE

The Italian excavations in the environs of Khaulān aṭ-Ṭiyāl (about 12-30 miles southeast of Sanaa)[8] have given us insight into the lifestyle and social structures of this civilization from approximately 2700 to 2000 B.C. or 2900 to 1800 B.C. However, de Maigret, one of the excavators, has pointed out that we have gained merely a minuscule glimpse and that many additional expeditions are necessary.

The population here was sedentary, subsisting on agriculture and livestock breeding. Evidence of beasts of burden might possibly confirm that goods were transported. Especially the existence of obsidian from sources beyond the borders of present-day Yemen is an indication that long distance trade took place.

Two types of settlements can be identified: smaller ones of less than a quarter acre and larger ones of more than 2.5 acres. The latter are in the valley and are separated from each other by a large and uniform distance. The smaller settlements situated in between indicate a society divided into separate family groups. The residential units were comprised of 3-4 houses built around a central common square where excavators found traces of fire and cooking sites as well as millstones. The larger settlement type is an indication, according to de Maigret, of a higher level of social organization: the transition from a purely farming village to a true center. At one site, based on the architecture of one room, excavators believe they discovered a type of meeting hall. A phallic idol that was found could have been used in a fertility rite, indicating some kind of religious practice. In de Maigret's opinion, the choice of geographic location for these settlements is what makes this Bronze Age civilization unique. It shows that the inhabitants already had considerable knowledge of hydrolics. They chose a region whose particular geological, pedological, and sedimentary conditions guaranteed a sufficient and convenient water supply. This view is supported by the German expeditions in the Mārib oasis. Immigration systems there trace back to the late third millennium B.C.

At various sites it was also possible to confirm the existence of individual workshops for the working of flint and obsidian. There was also a ceramics industry. Despite certain similarities in architecture, masonry, and ceramics production with other ancient Middle Eastern civilizations, de Maigret has emphasized expressly the autochtonous nature of this Bronze Age civilization in Yemen. He has also pointed out that French expeditions north of the Wadi al-Jauf also discovered Bronze Age settlements.

On the basis of pottery from other sites dated in the second half of the second millennium B.C., de Maigret believes that this Bronze Age civilization in northern Yemen existed throughout the entire second millennium B.C. In any case, the artifacts found in the Khaulān aṭ-Ṭiyāl region clearly show that this civilization had already made the transition from a simple family economy to a more complex societal form with a wide range of activities.

Settlements in the Khaulān aṭ-Ṭiyāl region were abandoned between roughly 2000 and 1800 B.C., according to de Maigret, for tectonic reasons. Changes led to increased fluctuation in the amount of precipitation, which caused the broad sedimentary plain that provided favorable farmland to wash away.

A short time later, around 1500 B.C., this general area seems to have been resettled in the lower lying valleys. This time, larger irrigation systems were set up. When following the course of Wadi Dhana in 1985, de Maigret discovered a large settlement called al-Markaba, which showed similarities neither to the Bronze Age settlements nor the Sabaean settlements that came later, starting around the tenth-ninth centuries.[9]

A German-Russian expedition in Ṣabir, in the Laḥej province (former South Yemen), which commenced in winter 1994-95, uncovered a Bronze Age coastal civilization that was totally unknown up to that time.[10] Excavators believe this civilization had extended from Abyan and Aden to Jīzān in the Saudi Arabian Tihāma. Ṣabir's heyday was in the second half of the second millennium B.C., but its origins might trace back to the early second millennium, if not even the late third millennium B.C. Two excavation campaigns yielded an inventory of artifacts that are unique in their diversity, according to the excavators. Ṣabir subsistence was based on agriculture, livestock breeding, fishing, and industrial production. According to B. Vogt, one of the excavators, the specimens found in Ṣabir are significant because they belonged to a "civilization" that directly preceded the classical ancient South Arabian cultures chronologically, but which displays no or at most very few cultural links to them. On the other hand, it shows strong connections to the preaxumitic sites in Abyssinia, Eritrea, and the Sudan. This assumption is supported by the paleoethobotanical investigations conducted by Italian researchers in the Yemenite highlands. L. Constantini[11] has maintained that Yemen was part of the original Abyssinian-Sudanese center.

2. THE (PROTO-)SABAEAN PERIOD

Regardless of whether or not there were mukarribs as early as the twelfth century B.C., the previously mentioned Italian excavation[12] (also under the leadership of de Maigret) near al-Durayb in Wadi Yalā, a tributary of the great Wadi Dhana, uncovered evidence of a much more advanced and specialized civilization.[13] De Maigret believes that this large complex in Wadi Yalā dates back to the tenth-ninth centuries B.C. One of the many investigations carried out in one of the houses ("structure A") yielded a calibrated C-14 dating of 1395-920 B.C.

These remarks show, on the one hand, that our knowledge of the structures of (proto-)Sabaean civilizations has been greatly enhanced through archaeological research conducted over the last ten years. On the other hand, however, additional meaningful inscriptions need to be found, in particular from the early period, in order to make statements any more specific than somewhat generally noting further development and differentiation.

Much more information is available on the "Mukarrib Period," that is, starting around the eighth century B.C. The Sabaean state was characterized by "ʾAlmaqah, Karibʾīl, and Sabaʾ,"[14] whereby the Sabaʾ tribe formed the center of the state. The mukarrib reigned over the Sabaean state and its tributaries. Although this state had a theocratic basis, and the mukarrib performed certain religious tasks,[15] he was not a "priest-king."[16] Rather, he was the political "unifier of the land." He led military operations and carried out building construction and other public projects. It is simply the case that religion was manifested also in these public projects. Beeston[17] commented on a text reporting on a strategic military operation that was carried out in agreement with a favorable omen from the chief tribal deity. It should also be noted that state structures and official functions—whether mukarrib or king—varied from kingdom to kingdom in South Arabia.[18]

If it can be assumed that for a certain period of time the title of mukarrib and king coexisted—though later on, the former fell totally into oblivion—then one might ask if there was a difference between the two titles, and if so, how did their functions differ. Based on inscriptions it has been shown there there was no difference in function. According to Beeston[19] this shift in title definitely did not reflect a change from a theocratic to a secular regime.

In addition to the mukarrib or king, the kabīr was also an important eponym. He carried out religious, economic, and political tasks. Various old South Arabian kingdoms were dated according to the kabīr's reign. These eponyms came from a variety of clans in Maʿīn and Qatabān, whereas in Sabaʾ the kabīr had to be a member of only certain clans.[20] The kabīr's position was later replaced by the "qayl." Qayls made up their own social class in the aristocracy.[21] Aside from these, there were numerous other official positions.[22] It is certain that the king ruled with the aid of certain officials and representatives of the people, such as the large landowners. One could speak of a "state council," whereby the king was not permitted to make decisions independently.[23]

The large landowners comprised one of the most important social classes.[24] In this context it should be said that land initially belonged to the god or the state. Since the land had to be farmed to bring in returns, it was then ceded to vassals or large landowners.

Aside from the large landowners, we also know of the soldier class,[25] traders, free peasants, and serfs (ʾdm)[26] as well as "slaves" (ʿabd).[27] In addition to the divisions listed here, there was another form of social stratification as described by Beeston.[28] It was based on the fact that old South Arabian civilization was founded predominantly upon a peasant population. In other words, the base of the pyramid was the village ("bait") and its community. The next higher social level was the connection between two or more villages into a unit, or tribe ("shaʿb"). Old South Arabian history shows that one such tribe would take control over other tribes for economic, political, or military reasons. This ended in the third level of the pyramid, the federation or commonwealth. Beeston has compared this with ancient Greece, where the "bait" corresponds to the demos ("community"), the "shaʿb" to the polis (such as Athens or Thebes), and the "commonwealth" to a union of several poleis, whereby one polis predominated, such as Athens or the Dorian League.[29]

Furthermore, Beeston[30] has indicated that with respect to the social institutions there was a distinct difference between highland and lowland regions in the Sabaean federation. The most significant cities in the lowlands, at least with respect to Mārib and Nashq, were, in the first few centuries A.D., a community of free burghers who owned the city and its environs. Other than their obligations toward the king, they were ruled only by a magistrate. In the mountains, on the other hand, there was a well-defined system of social stratification. Every community was ruled by an aristocratic family and these referred to themselves as the "qayls of the community." This brief description of the social structures is based on inscriptions, though it must be kept in mind that to today large gaps remain in the total picture.

VII. The Economy at the Time of Ancient South Arabia

The word "economy" evokes images of trade, frankincense and myrrh, and the famous incense route. One must keep in mind, however, that the significance of this profitable trade had decreased greatly as an overland route for the individual South Arabian kingdoms, at the latest with the decline of the Minaean kingdom.[1] Once insight had been gained into the monsoon winds, this trading shifted to the sea route. This sea trade with incense—and often even with other goods instead—was another important aspect of the ancient South Arabian economy.

Finally, the third pillar of the economy was agriculture. The Ṣayhad civilization, that is, the states lying adjacent to the Ramlat Ṣayhad (Ramlat as-Sabʿatayn) desert,[2] was predominantly an "irrigation culture" of settled farmers.[3]

1. OVERLAND TRADE

Profits for the various old South Arabian kingdoms from frankincense and myrrh trade were based, first of all, on the fact that these resins were from trees native to this region[4] or, to be more precise, to the central part of the South Arabian coastal region. Second, the wealthy overseers of the routes charged exorbitant fees to those transporting goods along the incense route, whether as payment of tolls, taxes in the form of incense for the temples, payment for lodgings, water, and animal feed, or "protection fees." G. Van Beek[5] attempted to calculate a cautious estimate for the price of incense, concluding that an industrial worker in the United States in 1960 would have had to work approximately one week for a pound of low quality incense and two weeks for the best quality. The price for myrrh was even double that of frankincense.[6]

The incense route was not a single road; in fact, there were several routes. Secondary roads led from the cultivation region and loading ports to the collection areas in the interior of the country. From the Dhofār incense region, which was part of the Ḥaḍramaut kingdom at that time, an overland route led to the capital city of Shabwa via Wadi Ḥaḍramaut. There was also a coastal route to the port of Qanaʾ, near Biʾr ʿAlī. From there the route continued to Maifaʿa and then on to Shabwa. This was the beginning of the actual "incense route," which then continued via Timnaʿ and Mārib to Najrān. East and southeast of Wadi Beiḥān, where Timnaʿ was located, were the regions where myrrh was cultivated, so it was possible to purchase or trade for myrrh along this route.

The route branched in Najrān. One fork ran parallel to the Red Sea via Yatrib (present-day Medina), Dedān (present-day al-ʿUlā), and al-Ḥijr (present-day Madain Salih) to Petra, capital of the Nabataean kingdom. There was a branch that led to Leuke Kome, the famous Rea Sea port. The main route, however, went from Petra across the Negev to Gaza at the Mediterranean. The other route led eastwards from Najrān through Wadi Duwāsir to al-Aflāğ and Hajar, finally ending in Gerrha at the Persian Gulf.

There is relatively little known about the regulations that governed overland trade. Some market regulations are known,[7] but these were primarily concerned with local trading matters and offer little information about the international trade that took place along the incense route, especially with the west. Nonetheless, from an inscription on the famous stela[8] at the Timnaʿ marketplace, we know that this site was to become a trading center, but that trade between individual village communities within Qatabān were subject to restrictions. This regulation served taxation purposes. Trade transactions at the marketplace in Timnaʿ could be far better monitored, thus making it difficult for traders to evade taxes and other fees. It was more difficult to control other forms of trade.

Also, distinctions were made between Qatabānian and non-Qatabānian traders. All merchants were required to pay a standard tax, but "foreign" merchants were charged additional fees as well.

Classical authors such as Theophrastus, Strabo, and Pliny offer considerable additional information on the international incense trade.[9]

2. TRADE BY SEA

Sea trade in the Red Sea and the Indian Ocean existed long before the emergence of the ancient South Arabian kingdoms. But the major breakthrough did not come until nautical insight made it possible for traders to take advantage of the patterns of the monsoon winds for seafaring.[10] This gave sea trading an enormous thrust,[11] and overland trade dwindled accordingly. Producers and importers started contacting each other directly, and many of the taxes that had been charged along the incense route were eliminated.

The increase in sea travel also profitted South Arabian harbors that served as intermediate stops or transfer points, or ones that participated in trading with their own fleets. The most significant South Arabian ports, according to the *Periplus* and Pliny (Nat. Hist. VI, xxvi, 104), were Muza (north of Mocha at the present site of Maušiğ[12]) and Okelis (at the Bab al-Mandab strait) along the Red Sea coast, and Qanaʾ (near present-day Biʾr ʿAlī) and Mocha, on the South Arabian coast.[13] Eudaemon Arabia (present-day Aden) was no longer significant at the time of the *Periplus* (probably first century A.D.)[14] because Roman seamen from Egypt had learned of the monsoon winds and sailed directly to India, eliminating Aden as an intermediate stop.[15] Furthermore, it is possible that the Romans under Augustus had destroyed Aden.[16]

Muza replaced Aden as a stopover port. Rome exported all kinds of goods, including textiles, metals, and food (wine, oil, grains), as well as luxury items such as gold and silver goods. In exchange,

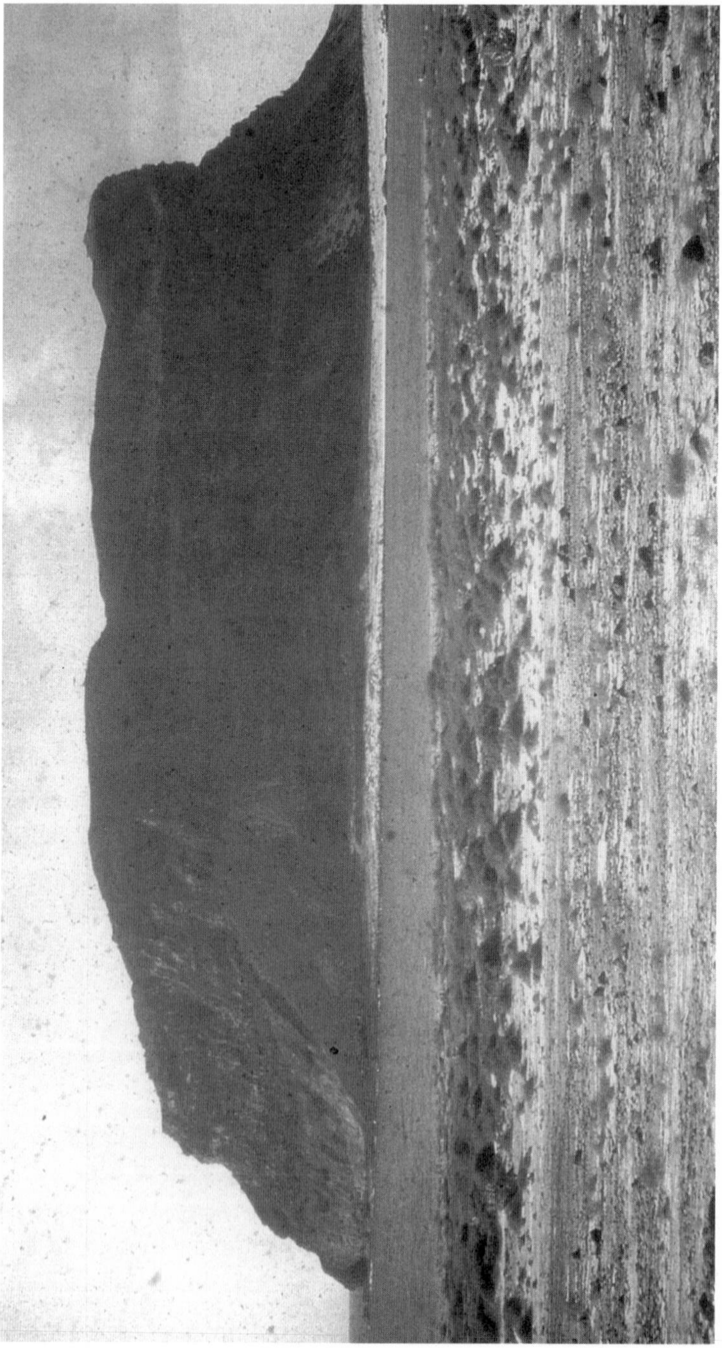

Qana’

Rome received primarily myrrh.[17] It should be noted here that not only luxury items were shipped to India. On the contrary, from the *Periplus* it is known that items of mass use were also shipped regularly.[18]

Ships from Muza itself headed for Africa trading goods—especially glasswares, iron tools, and weapons—for ivory, shells, and rhinoceros horns.[19] The most famous southern market, Rhapta,[20] was mentioned in the *Periplus*. There it said that this area, called Azania, was an overseas colony of the Sabaeans and the Ḥimyarites. Rhapta itself, however, was supposedly put under the administration of merchants of Muza.

Whereas trading activities in Muza functioned mostly by private initiative, in Qanaʾ trade was subject to strict goverment control.[21] Muza was a trade center for myrrh; in Qanaʾ, the main item of trade was frankincense. Other than that, trade was similar in the two ports. In the *Periplus*[22] it was reported that Qanaʾ was involved in intensive trading with the Romans in Egypt as well as with ports in Africa, southern Iran, and India. The imported goods were basically the same as those imported to Muza.

Sea trading with China also took place,[23] although most of this trade took place along the various roads comprising the famous "silk road." From South China, overland routes went through Assam and Burma to the Indian ports of Barbaricon at the mouth of the Indus and Barygaza in the Gulf of Cambay. The primary Chinese exports were Chinese cinnamon—cassia—and silk, which was then processed in Syria and Egypt.

Summarizing, with respect to both overland and sea trading, for centuries South Arabia played an important role in trade between east and west, due to the availability of frankincense and myrrh, and because it had several significant ports and controlled many of the overland routes.

3. AGRICULTURE

Although the first two sections of this chapter might give the impression that land and sea trading alone made up the "backbone" of the ancient South Arabian economy, it must be emphasized—as already mentioned in the introduction to this chapter—that a majority of the ancient South Arabian population were peasants. They were not bedouins but organized into tribal associations. Agriculture was always the primary aspect of economic life. Striking evidence of this are the magnificent irrigation systems, not only in Mārib but also elsewhere in ancient South Arabia. U.S. excavations and surveys in 1950-52 in the Beiḥān region, that is, within the Qatabānian kingdom, uncovered extensive irrigation systems.[24] The French excavations that took place starting in 1975 in and around Shabwa, capital of the Ḥaḍramaut kingdom, should also be mentioned in this regard, where impressive irrigation systems were also discovered.[25]

Horst Kopp, a leading expert on Yemenite agriculture, correctly emphasized[26] that there is a long tradition of farming in Yemen. Because there were diverse water sources to take advantage of, and by applying knowledge of them when building the well-known terraces, peasants were able to cultivate even remote mountainous areas. Kopp noted that additional characteristics of Yemenite agriculture include the cultivation of seeds using choice selection, fertilization in conjunction with the widespread practice of cattle breeding in cowsheds, and efficient use of minimal resources. Due to the isolation of the mountainous regions, many ancient working methods and tools were still used although they had long since fallen out of use elsewhere in the world. The main tools for working the soil were a cattle-drawn plow with a simple spike, a hoe, and a share. The last-named was a board with chains attached that was also pulled by cattle.[27]

The main crops were, then as now, millet and later wheat, barley, corn, dates, and vegetables.[28] With respect to antiquity, this information is based on knowledge gained from the German expeditions in the Mārib oasis as well as the evaluation of inscriptions from the Sabaean period. One inscription (CIH 540), for example, a supply list, indicated that workers helping to rebuild the Mārib dam in 449-450 A.D. received wheat and barley. This and another inscription (CIH 541) reported that the amount of grape wine consumed by the workers in 440 A.D. amounted to roughly 430 camel-loads, as opposed to 200 loads of date wine. In 450 A.D. all 670 camel-loads were grape wine. The plant culture mentioned most often in inscriptions was probably palms. We also know from inscriptions that there was extensive livestock breeding. Farmers needed animals for the work in the fields and in addition animals were used for transportation purposes, such as when the Mārib dam was repaired.[29]

Kopp stressed that Yemenite agriculture is still essentially a subsistence economy, that is, most of the agricultural products were and are for the farmers' own use.

In closing, it should once again be underlined that ancient South Arabian agriculture was very highly developed. Inscriptions indicate diversified terminology for types of soil and plants. A large number of so-called peasant inscriptions have also been found. These are requests that the fields be protected or that they thrive, or offering thanks to the gods for a good harvest.[30]

VIII. The Military

Unfortunately, no major reports are available on the military in South Arabia. Our knowledge is based on inscriptions reporting on military campaigns and battles.[1] It is thus not surprising that recent works on ancient South Arabia do not have a chapter devoted to the military.[2] Exceptions are a lengthy essay by Beeston[3] and the 1994 work by J.-F. Breton in the *Archäologische Berichte aus dem Yemen* series published by the German Archaeological Institute in Sanaa.[4] The latter work deals exclusively with one aspect, that is, fortresses in old South Arabia from the seventh to the first centuries B.C.

War certainly played an important role in life back then. This is apparent, for example, when glancing at the *Sabaic Dictionary* by A. F. L. Beeston, M. A. Ghul, W. W. Müller, and J. Ryckmans. There are some 120 words that are directly associated with the military, especially war. Beeston's essay also refers to numerous words and expressions in the Old South Arabic language dealing with this subject.

Because of terrain conditions in South Arabia, it can be assumed that the type of warfare waged there differed from that waged elsewhere, in Mesopotamia for instance, at the same time.[5] Thus chariots were hardly used at all. Siege machines too were largely unknown in South Arabia as was the use of cavalry to any great extent.

Beeston[6] distinguished between three groups of soldiers within the so-called *Ṣayhad* states, that is, the states adjacent to the Ramlat Ṣayhad (present-day Ramlat as-Sabʿatayn) desert. The "Khamis"[7] comprised the main army. They were under the direct command of the king or one of his generals and were strictly national troops; in other words, no Ḥimyarites were allowed to serve with the Sabaean Khamis. There is disagreement[8] whether the Khamis were career soldiers or whether it was comprised of peasants, like the Roman army at the time of the republic, who returned to the fields after the campaign was concluded.

The second group were the levied troops, mustered by the highland communities. They fought under the direct command of their *qayl*.[9] These two groups formed the main force of the army. The third group named by Beeston was the cavalry, though he concedes that in terms of number they were not very significant. One inscription, for example, refers to a campaign of the Ḥimyar general Saʿadtaʾ lab Yatlaf around 315 A.D. against the Ḥaḍramaut kingdom. The total strength of the army was 670 warriors, 20 of which were regular cavalry and there were another fifty horsemen.[10]

In addition, every army—especially the Sabaean and Ḥaḍramitic ones—was reinforced with bedouin mercenaries.[11]

The size of the respective army varies according to the different inscriptions. Once a figure of 2500 is mentioned, another time it was 670 warriors, and then figures of 270, 203, and 1026. One inscription reports of 2000 casualties in the Ḥaḍramaut army. Another mentions 4000 soldiers who defended Shabwa. Most of the time the number of soldiers is listed as under one thousand. There is one, albeit questionable, source that mentions 16,000 nonregular Ḥimyar soldiers who were chased off by only 1500 warriors and 40 mounted troops.[12]

The main weapons used were the dagger and the lance. Beeston[13] has claimed that the bow was often used in Arabia for hunting, but not as a weapon. I am not convinced that this was the case. One should not forget that this was one of the primary weapons used by the Parthians, who were relatively close both geographically and chronologically. For example, the bow was responsible for the Parthian victory in the famous battle of Karrhae (present-day Harran, Turkey) in 53 B.C. against the Romans under Crassus. It should also be noted that the composite bow, which appeared in the course of the fourth century B.C., developed on the Arabian peninsula.[14] Moreover, in the necropolis of Wadi Dura (Ḥaḍramaut), a fragment of a copper bowl was found that was adorned with an illustration of a bow and quiver.[15]

Beeston also views the sword as a weapon seldom used in antiquity. In Arabia it was a rare and precious weapon used only by chieftains.

Something that does not appear at all on Beeston's list of weapons used in South Arabia is the sling, though it was a primary weapon as early as prehistoric times. Strabo[16] reported of its use by the Arabs of the western Arabian peninsula. In the early sixteenth century A.D. about 3000 Egyptian mercenaries served in the Sultan's army; in addition to the sword and lance, they also used the sling.[17]

Regarding the strategic goals of the Sabaean-Ḥimyar confederation, according to Beeston[18] they focussed on two things: conquering important towns and carrying out pincer movements, in which the troops were divided into two columns, thus confronting the enemy from two directions. To these aims, Breton[19] added a third: the destruction of vitally necessary irrigation systems.

The type of warfare practiced can be surmised from the type of fortresses built. Breton[20] has distinguished between three eras of defense systems in South Arabia: the early historical period, though the starting date is uncertain; the so-called Mukarrib Period (seventh-sixth centuries B.C.), and finally, the period in which major defensive construction projects were discontinued (first century B.C.).

In the first era, defense walls were made of roughly cut stone and their courses were irregular. There is some evidence of casemate walls,[21] but walls formed by adjoining buildings *(edifices contigus)* were more common.

The second era coincides with the beginning of "South Arabian" civilization. It shows a change in fortress construction. During this time great joined walls started being built. The prime example of this is Mārib, where the wall is roughly 4200 m. (2.6 miles) long and includes several different wall types: clay brick walls with and without limestone planking, or with facings of reused architectural elements, tuff walls, or lava walls.[22] Four city gates and numerous towers could also be identified. This blossoming of fortress architecture, including increasing the height of city walls to 26 feet in Maʿīn and up to 46 feet in Barāqish, is a sign of prosperity, according to Breton,[23] and not an indication that siege techniques had been further developed. High agricultural proceeds and income from the caravan trade supported this upswing in fortress architecture.

The third era started in the first century B.C.[24] Breton noted a decrease in construction projects for military purposes. The walls were no longer maintained or repaired. The reasons for this varied from region to region. In the Minaean kingdom, it was due to a shift in trade from overland to sea routes, and thus a drop in income. In other areas it was caused by attacks by nomadic groups. Conventional fortress walls were useless against such enemies. Walls of unfired clay bricks in Mārib illustrate the city's decline in the first century B.C. In Qatabān, no defense systems appear to have been built since the second century B.C. Only in Ḥaḍramaut could some construction up to the third century A.D. be identified based on excavations in Shabwa.

Summarizing, it can be said that warfare and siege techniques were not nearly as refined and developed in South Arabia as they were in Rome and the Hellenistic states or the kingdoms in Mesopotamia and Asia Minor.[25] Wars in South Arabia seemed more like wars between individual tribes. One explanation for this could be that South Arabia was a relatively remote region that encountered "foreign" warfare methods, especially siege techniques, only once, that is, during the Roman campaign under Aelius Gallus in 25-24 B.C.

IX. Religion(s) in Ancient South Arabia

Old South Arabic inscriptions mention a wealth of gods. Religion dominated private and public life.[1] One could basically speak of a theocratic society.[2] Our knowledge of religious practices, however, is very limited. The uncovered temples do not reveal the contents of the beliefs of their builders; it is only the inscriptions that offer any information of this kind. Beeston[3] was not mistaken in noting that an analysis of these inscriptions is like trying to reconstruct the religion of the Greeks solely on the basis of Greek inscriptions, without being able to refer to any literary sources, which are very important in understanding religious ideas. In the case of Yemen, there is only one extant text that could be regarded as "literary."[4]

The pantheon of ancient South Arabia was polytheistic. It stands out as being predominantly astral in character, as were other religions in the ancient Middle East. The chief deity in Saba', Ma'īn, Qatabān, and 'Ausān was "'Attar,"[5] the male god of Venus. Only in Ḥaḍramaut was he called "'Astar." His high status can perhaps be explained in that 'Attar was closely tied to irrigation, that is, the most vital issue to the old South Arabian kingdoms.[6] The name corresponds to the female "Ishtar" of Mesopotamia or the Syrian-Palestinian "Astarte." We also know of a sun deity, Shams, which was a male god called Shamash in Assyria. The trinity was completed with a moon god,[7] named 'Almaqah, 'Ilmaqah, or Ilumquh in Saba'.[8] He was the national deity there; in Ma'īn and 'Ausān he was known by the name Wadd, in Qatabān he was 'Amm, and in Ḥaḍramaut, Sīn.[9]

According to Beeston,[10] it is an oversimplification to see this trinity as merely a symbolic representation of Venus, moon, and sun.[11] The true context is presumably at least as complex as the prevailing religious systems in Mesopotamia and Syria at that time.

In addition to these chief deities, there were numerous other subordinate gods in the various South Arabian kingdoms. In terms of number, the tutelary gods were also very significant for a certain city, tribe,[12] clan, or family. Some gods also served a specific function. For instance, the gods Munaḍḍiḥ and Munaḍḍiḥat protected the irrigation systems and the borders. Ḥalfān was the god of the oath and Mutībqabṭ was a Minaean god of the harvest. Robin[13] has also referred to the significance of the mountains for the ancient South Arabian religion, reporting that recently found inscriptions reveal the existence of two mountains worshipped as deities.

The gods were often represented by animal symbols, such as the snake for Wadd, or the bull as the animal symbol for ʾAlmaqah. Frequently, deities were also represented using an abstract symbol at the beginning or end of the inscription. For example, a club was the symbol for ʾAlmaqah and a lightning bolt symbolized the Qatabānian god ʿAmm. Expert opinions diverge on whether or not idols or statues existed in human form.[14]

The "home" or "residence" of the gods was the temple.[15] The temple was very important, not only in religious life, but generally in public life as well. Its status and significance can be roughly compared to that of the Sumerian temple in Mesopotamia in the fourth-third millennia B.C. There must have been a great number of temples, but Pliny's (Nat. Hist., book VI, xxxii, 154, 155) figures—that there were 65 temples in Timnaʿ and 67 in Shabwa—are perhaps somewhat too high.

The temples had considerable wealth. Their income came from duties and taxes as a result of the extensive land they owned and the collection of tithes (Nat. Hist., book XII, xxxii, 63), as well as religious offerings. Priests and/or officials took care of temple administration and business. The priests were also responsible for consulting the oracle and performing sacrifices. The priest class was inherited, with priesthood being passed down from generation to generation.[16]

There were also laypeople in the service of the temple. In addition to animal and drink offerings, we are also familiar with the ritual meal. In the previously mentioned inscription RES 4176[17] the god Taʾlab of Riyam ordered his tribe to carry out ritual meals. It cannot be determined with certainty whether or not there were human sacrifices.[18] Several inscriptions also report of ritual hunts for animals that were sacred to a certain god, such as the antilope to the god ʿAṯtar.[19]

There is little known about what was inside the temples, as the excavations have not offered much information in this regard. Various types of altars have been found, such as ones for sacrificing animals or for incense, whereby these altars had a wide variety of forms.

Concerning the cult of the dead, excavations[20] have offered some insight and confirm the wealth of form of burial monuments, as are familiar from other parts of the Arabian peninsula, such as Oman, Bahrain, and the United Arab Emirates. Here I shall mention only the excavations by G. Caton Thompson in 1938 in Ḥaḍramaut, the American excavations under the leadership of F. P. Albright in Wadi Beiḥān and Mārib in 1950-52, and the German expeditions under J. Schmidt[21] in the Mārib area. Known types of tombs include circular tumulus tombs, beehive tombs,[22] rectangular stone tombs with a circular burial chamber, so-called pillbox[23] tombs, as well as cave tombs[24] and burial towers. With respect to number, there were single graves, graveyards, and entire necropolises.[25]

The polytheistic form of religion described here was gradually replaced by monotheism in the fourth century, at least among the upper classes.[26] The various deities were abandoned in favor of Raḥmānān, the "merciful," the "ruler of the heavens." As mentioned previously, there is disagreement among researchers as to the form of monotheism practiced.[27] In addition to opinions that it was a form of Christianity or Judaism, it is also possible that Raḥmānism was neither of the two, but rather an authochtinous monotheism. Followers were *ḥunafāʾ* (singular *ḥanīf*), which basically means "one who has the true and pure religion."[28]

Whether or not the Jewish religion had gained a foothold before the reign of the Jewish king Yusuf Asʿar Yaṭʿar (Dhū Nuwās) in the early fifth century cannot be proven beyond a doubt. While some inscriptions indicate this, no other evidence exists.[29]

The same is true for Christianity. There is no convincing evidence that true Christianity existed in South Arabia before the sixth century.[30] It was not until the Abyssinians conquered the country in 525 A.D. that this religion was "imposed" on the people. The term "Raḥmānān" appears in the mid-sixth century as an epithet for the first person in the Christian trinity. Even after the country was Islamized, Christianity continued in South Arabia for a long time, albeit in a process of decline.[31]

In closing, it can be said that because religion penetrated all aspects of life of the individual and society as a whole, it was not difficult for Islam to assert itself in South Arabia in the seventh century. Muhammad himself supposedly said, "Faith is Yemenite, wisdom is Yemenite, and Islam is Yemenite."[32]

X. The Art of South Arabia

To today it remains difficult to offer an overview of art in ancient South Arabia. Materials are lacking with which to conduct a comprehensive analysis and make any conclusive statements. This becomes obvious in comparison with publications on Mesopotamian art. There are countless general descriptions of the art of Mesopotamia and a flood of specific studies. The situation is very different regarding South Arabia. Archaeologists dealing with this subject can make reference to a large number of philological and historical works, but there are very few archaeological investigations that treat works of art.[1] It would be pointless to "blame" anyone in particular for this state of affairs, as the external conditions in the country alone represent a significant obstacle. We can only hope that with the end of the tragic civil war there will now be greater opportunities for archaeological field research to be conducted within the country.

In contrast to Mesopotamia, where conditions there supported construction largely with clay bricks, building engineers and architects in ancient South Arabia were fortunate to have sufficient stone at their disposal. This was especially true in northern Yemen; in southern Yemen, that is, ancient Ḥaḍramaut, the situation was not quite as favorable.

1. ARCHITECTURE

a) Secular buildings

Although a great number of city names have been passed down,[2] the visible remains of these cities are not all that impressive. Despite the fact that excavations have furthered our knowledge in this area, visitors to Mārib or Maʿīn would certainly be more taken by the religious structures—for example, the temples—than by the secular structures. The city walls, such as in Maʿīn or Mayfaʿa, on the other hand, are truly impressive sights.

Let it be said from the outset that truly informative investigations and maps are still scarce. This is because sites were often examined only superficially or sketches were drawn up based on inadequate aerial photographs. In addition, many city walls or other structures have over time become victims of "progress," when building materials were reused for modern buildings. And finally, two civil wars have done their part as well.

It has been generally determined that the built-up areas of these cities were relatively small as compared with other locations in the ancient Middle East. The largest city in ancient South Arabia, Mārib, covered a land area of 272 acres (110 hectares).[3] All other cities of any significance were even smaller in area: Timnaʿ was about 56-59 acres (23 or 24 ha).[4] and Shabwa was about 37 acres (15 ha).[5] In contrast, Babylon covered 2100 acres (850 ha)[6]; Niniveh, 1850 acres (750 ha),[7] and even Ctesiphon, the Sasanid capital, was 1335 acres (540 ha) in area.[8] It must be taken into account that these other cities were all in Mesopotamia, which was a largely flat region, and they could grow and expand more or less without limits. In South Arabia on the other hand, it was necessary to adapt to the land to a greater extent. This was more comparable to Bogazköy in Anatolia, the capital of the Hittites, which was built on uneven terrain. The size of this city covered about 415 acres (168 ha).[9]

Often, but not always, the city settlements were rectangular. They were frequently built in valley basins on a natural or artifically built-up elevation. This was probably done to avoid the dangers of flooding due to the *sayls* (occasional flash floods, mostly in arid wadis).

Māʿin

Thulla: cistern

Some examples of this type of city are Mārib, Ṣirwāḥ, Maʿīn, and Timnaʿ.[10]

Towns were sometimes built below fortresses that could serve as protection in times of emergency, such as Ẓafār, the capital of the Ḥimyar kingdom, built below the often-mentioned fortress Raydān; or Thulla (roughly 30 mi. north of Sanaa); or Qanaʾ, with its fortress Ḥusn al-G͟hurāb ("raven fortress"), built high above the well-known frankincense port.

Of course there were a large number of cities, a majority in fact, that were protected by their own thick city walls. Mārib is the prime example of such a city, with its approximately 2.6 mile (4200 m) long city wall,[11] divided into numerous curtains and bastions, towers, and city gateways.[12] The same is true for Shabwa, which even had two defensive walls surrounding it.[13]

Next to nothing is known about the palaces mentioned in inscriptions.[14] The single, praiseworthy exception is the French excavation in Shabwa, where researchers were able to uncover most of the so-called Chateau Royal in six campaigns from 1980 to 1985.[15]

It has not been determined conclusively[16] whether the "Timnaʿ Temple 1," uncovered by an American expedition in 1950-51, is perhaps not a temple at all, but also a palace, as Breton[17] maintains. In any case, its size, architecture, and the building methods used greatly resemble the "chateau" in Shabwa.

The height of ancient South Arabian secular architecture was displayed in the irrigation works, of which the Mārib dam enjoys pride of place. Irrigation of the soil was the decisive prerequisite for the thriving agriculture and thus the survival of the country. It therefore goes virtually without saying that the architects and building engineers of South Arabia in antiquity made great achievements in this field. As has been said previously,[18] other irrigation systems were built in Mārib long before the famous dam.

There has been so much written about these systems that I will limit discussion here to a minimum.[19] The dam was already known in antiquity far beyond the borders of South Arabia as a wonder of the world. Determining when it was built depends on the respective "chronological viewpoint" of the observer. Based on the "Long

Thulla

Chronology," which is the predominant opinion today, it was started in the sixth century B.C.[20] The dam was built because the older irrigation works in the Mārib oasis from the late third millennium B.C. no longer sufficed. The area to be irrigated had grown to such an extent that the existing facilities were insufficient. The Wadi Dhana was blocked at its narrowest point and an approximately 2000 ft. dam was built.[21] It was made of soil and sediment covered with rough stone and mortar, reaching a height of 60 ft. and having a base thickness of almost 200 ft. At the northern and southern ends, two huge sluices were built, the northern one being the larger of the two. Water distribution channels connected to these sluices transported water to the fields. In all, an area of roughly 37 sq. mi. was irrigated in this way. The dam was primarily intended as a catchment for the floodwaters of the *sayls,* which reached the dam at high speeds; here the water was slowed down and distributed. Schmidt[22] mentioned peak run-off velocities of over 35,000 cu. ft. per sec., and in extreme cases, the floods could even reach flows of 60,000 cu. ft. per sec. The entire complex was thought through to the last detail; in other words, it was a masterpiece of ancient building design and engineering craftsmanship. A more or less intact state was necessary to ensure that the dam functioned properly, since if any problems arose, such as a collapse or break, orders from above were necessary in organizing the large numbers of people needed to repair it. When the dam broke for the second time in 450 A.D., 20,000 men were employed to carry out the repairs. Even when there was another break in 542, it was possible to repair the dam. The final catastrophe occurred between 575 and 580, marking the end of this "wonder of the world," because the Sabaeo-Ḥimyar kingdom was in its decline.[23] Once again, the irrigation systems of Timnaʿ and Shabwa shall be mentioned here.[24] In addition to these major facilities, there were also countless smaller works including wells, cisterns, and dams[25] that served irrigation purposes.

Another aspect of architecture were the roads.[26] The Mablaqah pass has pride of place in this regard, connecting Wadi Beiḥān and Wadi Ḥarib, in the Qatabān kingdom. The pass is a paved road, 3-4 miles long and 10-12 feet wide. The pavement consisted of very large stones with a curb. The vertex of the pass was carved into the rock,

Mārib: northern sluice

Mārib: dam

extending over a distance of 100 feet and a depth of 30 feet. N. S. I. Groom,[27] whose report has been referred to here, assumed that this road was one of the main roads along the incense route.[28] Not far away, there was another, albeit smaller, paved road in Wadi Ḥarib that led through the Najd-Marqad pass.[29] Other roads are known, many of which certainly marked the ancient course of the incense route.[30]

In connection with the roads, the walls blocking these roads that were discovered should also be mentioned. The best example of one of these walls is at Libna,[31] north of the port of Qanaʾ. An inscription (RES 2687)[32] in the gateway explains its purpose. It was build by a Ḥaḍramite ruler as protection against the Ḥimyarites, who had conquered the important Qanaʾ harbor. There is disagreement with respect to the dating of the inscription, ranging from the fifth to the third centuries B.C. to 10 B.C.[33] The wall is approximately 540 feet long and fifteen feet high.[34] It was made of well-cut limestone blocks[35] and had only one gate. Von Wissmann and Doe also tell of other smaller blockade walls.[36]

In conclusion, it must be said of the secular architecture of ancient South Arabia that the architects and engineers of the time accomplished amazing feats. Especially impressive is the diversity in form.

b) Religious architecture

Of all the architectural monuments, the temples are certainly among the most significant, especially since they are relatively well-preserved. Nevertheless, as J. Schmidt[37] correctly regrets, the present inventory of existing monuments is far from sufficient in drawing up a comprehensive description. For this reason, the classification based on types of ground plan sketches that Grohmann published in 1963[38] should be taken with a grain of salt. In 1988 M. Jung[39] also attempted to create a typological classification of the religious structures in South Arabia. Jung had access to a larger number of religious buildings, since the situation researchers were faced with had improved over the twenty-five years since Grohmann's work, and he was thus able to make more specific and differentiating statements. He too, however, had to admit that major gaps in our knowledge remain. Jung's system of dating is still based on the "Short Chronology,"[40]

Temple in Māʾin

which is no longer widely accepted. He generally followed Schmidt's classification of the temples, but divided these into more detailed subcategories.

It should generally be kept in mind that the magnificent temple complexes were preceded by more simple precursors that also served religious purposes. Schmidt[41] was certainly correct in drawing some parallels to the development of the irrigation systems and thus dating religious architecture as beginning in the third or, at the latest, the second millennium B.C. He suggested that these early religious monuments were located in the mountain ranges west of Mārib and the high-lying valleys, extending into the interior of the mountainous region, that is, the areas outside the cities along the major travel routes.[42]

Stela-type monoliths or stone formations were probably among the first monument types.[43] Jung[44] classified this early stage as "rock sanctuaries." Later, these monuments were enclosed, forming a "sacred precinct." Another stage in the classification system distinguishes between structures with a divided or an undivided ground plan, whereby these had either one or more rooms.[45] Characteristic of all of these was a hypaethral design, i.e., they had a roofless central space. This developed into a form that Schmidt called a "canonical type of classical Sabaean temple."[46] Its basic form was a closed, rectangular construction with a dominant hypaethral central space surrounded by a colonnade and a three-part cella. Materials and techniques were both already more developed in this phase. As examples Schmidt mentioned the temple at Wadd (between Mārib and Ṣirwāḥ),[47] which he dated as the early seventh century B.C., and the temple dedicated to the god ʾAlmaqah at Masājid (about 17 mi. south of Mārib),[48] which Schmidt believed to be an imitation of the Wadd temple.

In Schmidt's view,[49] the well-known ʾAwwām temple in Mārib is also one of these Sabaean temple types,[50] though he based his classification only on the presumably oldest parts of the structure. He also placed the so-called Barʾān Temple (present-day arsh-Bilqīs or al-ʿAmāʾid), with its five monolithic pillars, in the group of Sabaean rectangular temples. For the last named, hopefully new insight will be

Mārib: ʾAwwām temple

provided by recent German excavations. According to B. Vogt,[51] the excavations uncovered the platform of the temple from the seventh century B.C. and, under the forecourt that had been added later, parts of the remains of an earlier structure.

Schmidt contrasted the Sabaean temple type[52] with one having a different ground plan and room scheme known primarily from the Minaean al-Jauf and, later, from Qatabān as well. There are two variants of the same basic ground plan. One is an undivided rectangular building with six to eight supporting columns. Exemplifying this type, Schmidt named the so-called city temple at Maᶜīn, with two rows of three supporting columns each, and the Ḥusn al-Qays structure[53] in Ḥaḍramaut, also with six columns. The other variant is the "many-pillared temple" with a nondirectional ground plan, often square, with multiple trusses and a large number of supporting columns. Some examples of this are the Minaean temple at ash-Shaqab[54] (near Barāqish) with thirty-five columns, and one in Ḥusn al-Qays with sixteen columns. The twelve-columned temple uncovered by an Italian expedition a few years ago in Barāqish (the ancient Yaṯill in the Minaean kingdom), which was dedicated to the god Nakraḥ, would also belong to this group.[55]

I believe that in addition to the two basic types suggested by Schmidt—the Sabaean hypaethral temple with an inner peristyle and three-part cella; and the Minaean type with a covered six-pillared structure or the "many-pillared temple"—there is a third, namely, the Ḥaḍramitic "terrace temple." In 1978-79 the French mission under the leadership of Breton[56] uncovered seven temples, all of which had a monumental stairway leading to an enclosed terrace, or temenos, on which the cella was located. The interior of the cella was divided the same way in all of these temples: on the narrow side of the building along the main axis of the cella was the entranceway, about 3 feet wide, and along the back wall there was a podium and two rows of columns. The structure as a whole was situated such that it could be seen from a long distance. The basic design with monumental entranceway, terrace, and cella clearly distinguish these seven sites from the Sabaean and Minaean temple types.

Schmidt has divided South Arabian religious architecture into

Mārib: ʾAwwām temple

three major stages, or style phases:[57] the early period, in which an independent form developed, followed by an era of perfecting the form to classical heights, and finally a period in which foreign influences became noticeable. During this third period, Hellenist-Roman forms increasingly influenced South Arabian art. Jung[58] also emphasized the Egyptian influence on South Arabian temple architecture. While it can generally be said that neighboring civilizations certainly exerted some influence, such a comparison should not be exaggerated. A comparison of the oval ʾAwwām temple in Mārib with structures in Zimbabwe, for example, is somewhat far-fetched. The same is true for the comparison with the famous temple oval in Khafadje in Mesopotamia.[59]

Because of known reference points in ancient art of the Mediterranean countries, according to Schmidt, this third period and its creations are the easiest to date and classify. With respect to the two earlier periods, however, much research has yet to be done. A generally binding chronology must be worked out that allows for classification of all the various monuments. Hopefully, the first step in this direction has been taken, now that the "Long Chronology" seems to have become generally accepted.

2. SCULPTURE

Al-Hamdani's book *Iklîl*[60] has reported of sculpture—statues and statuettes[61]—in ancient South Arabia. Unfortunately very few sculptures are extant. Many of those in existence today were either discovered by chance or at improperly conducted excavations, making it difficult for the respective layer to be determined precisely. Of course, debate on the different chronologies has also prevented an exact absolute dating. K. Parlasca[62] mentioned in this context the dating of the well-known bronze horse in the Dumbarton Oaks Collection, which ranges from the sixth-fifth centuries B.C. to the fifth-sixth centuries A.D.[63]

In assessing these problems, it must first of all be assumed that ancient South Arabia never belonged politically to the Hellenistic states or the Roman Empire. The only time a foreign power tried to gain a foothold in South Arabia was the Roman campaign of Aelius Gallus in 25-24 B.C. As is known, this attempt failed. The temporary victories over South Arabia by the Abyssinians and the Persians shall not be considered here, as they took place at the close of old South Arabian history. However, this does not mean that the art of this region was therefore "purely" South Arabian, whatever that might be taken to mean. Through overland and sea trade, South Arabia developed relations with the Mediterranean countries[64] and with India. These relations and connections had lasting cultural and artistic impact. Hence among artifacts there are some imported articles as well as some demonstrating artistic influence from outside the region. Just as with dating, however, evaluations here vary greatly. In other words, the problems in analyzing ancient South Arabian art are numerous and complex.

The most well-known examples of large South Arabian sculpture are doubtless the two larger-than-life bronze statues (2.37 m and 2.38 m, approx. 7.8 ft.) that were uncovered at the excavation of the former crown prince Sayf al-Islām Aḥmad in Nakhlat al-Ḥamrāʾ (south of the Jabal Kanin and east of the Sanaa-Damar road). At the time they were mere fragments; now they are the showpieces of the National Museum in Sanaa. How did this happen? Through a cultural aid agreement between Yemen and the Federal Republic of Germany. The fragments were restored and connected in five years of work at the main Roman-Germanic museum in Mainz, Germany.[65] The statues are unclothed figures depicting two Ḥimyar rulers, a father and son. The inscriptions on the two statues inform us that the father was King Dhamarʿalī Yuhabirr, and he donated these figures to three men belonging to the same clan.

Most interesting, however, are two other inscriptions on the knees of the statue of the son that became visible in the course of the restoration in Mainz. One was written in the Greek language using the Greek alphabet. It says that a Greek artist named Phokas made the statue. The other inscription is in Sabaic; it names the local assistant Lahayʿamm, who put together the parts of the statue.[66] The dating of the two statues varies depending on the opinion of the respective scholar, ranging from the second century to the end of the third century A.D.[67]

This is unique in that it represents a joint project of a Greek and a local artist.[68] It can be assumed that these statues were made in South Arabia, whereby Phokas must have been a "traveling laborer," that is, a Greek-speaking artist, perhaps from the eastern part of the Roman empire.[69] There was a long tradition of metal casting in South Arabia,[70] thus it need not be assumed that the statue had been imported. Numerous other works of metal that were found at excavations confirm this tradition. Most of the other large and small sculptures found were uncovered by the American expeditions in Timnaʿ and Mārib. Recently, several bronze pieces were found by French expeditions in Shabwa.[71]

Regardless of whether the statues were large or small, they often showed the influence of "foreign" precursors. The two statues described above clearly correspond to the style commonly used to portray Roman emperors. The bronze statues that were found in the entrance hall of the ʾAwwām temple in Mārib,[72] on the other hand, display Cypro-Phoenician influence.[73] The sculptures found in Timnaʿ are also examples of foreign influence, such as the well-known pair of lions being ridden by unclothed boys. These have been the subject of much scholarly debate. Hellenistic influences are obvious here,[74] though the lion pair was most likely produced within the country, as suggested by the South Arabic inscriptions at the base. The list of examples where foreign influence is apparent can be easily extended. There have also been finds in which it is more or less clear that the items had been imported, such as the statuette of a Spartan warrior that was sighted in 1939 at al-Barīra in Ḥaḍramaut. It then disappeared into a private collection and reappeared in 1986 at a London auction. This figure, which has been dated to the second half of the sixth century B.C. was probably produced in a Spartan workshop.[75] Another example is the bronze statue of a dancer, which was found in Khōr Rōrī, the ancient Sumhuram on the coast of present-day Oman. It was without a doubt imported from India.[76]

Aside from bronze, alabaster was also commonly used in sculpture. The alabaster heads, such as those on display at the Museum of

Islamic Art in Berlin,[77] are classical old South Arabian works. They are characterized by basic cubic forms with sparing sculptural intervention and isolated facial features, conveying a timeless image of the person portrayed. Almut Hauptmann–von Gladiss mentioned standard presentations facing forward toward the observer. She saw connections to traditional Egyptian sculpture, with its basic cubic form, as well as a Parthian-Palmyrene influence.[78] Last but not least a find in Mārib should be mentioned, which included fifteen full sculpture marble bulls or bull's heads.[79]

3. SMALLER WORKS OF ART

This section includes a wide variety of works of art[80] such as alabaster grave stelae, marble and alabaster busts, bas-reliefs, bucraniums, capitals within an architectural structure, metal bowls, jewelry, glyptic, and wall paintings.[81] The necropolis discovered in 1984 at Hajar am-Dhaybiyya in Wadi Ḍurāʾ (Ḥaḍramaut) should be mentioned here.[82] The sensational finds made at this site have provided great insight into the art of ancient South Arabia.

The observations and statements made by French excavators in Shabwa are also very interesting in this context. Compared to earlier excavations, this expedition, which lasted from 1975 to 1987, was carried out under very different conditions and with different aims. This is not said as a criticism of the methods used by earlier expeditions, but is merely intended to emphasize that excavation techniques, methods, and perspectives have developed over time. Archaeology in Mesopotamia is a prime example of this.

Different chronological phases of foreign influence on art, and impact on other fields can be recognized in ancient Shabwa.[83] Ornamentation, ceramics, iconography, and coins, for instance, showed greater foreign influence than did religion, city planning, or building methods.

With respect to a chronological classification of these artistic works, the present state of research is far from being able to identify the historical development of the various forms of these smaller works of art. This would require in particular more stratigraphical excavations, which would enable absolute chronological data. Nevertheless, the French attempt in this direction represents an important first step. Many years ago, C. Rathjens[84] attempted to categorize a number of portrait heads now located in the Hamburg Museum of Ethnology. However, A. Hauptmann–von Gladiss[85] was not incorrect in stating that although Rathjens was able to determine different stages of sculpture, he did not succeed in providing a basis for the historical development of ancient South Arabian sculpture.

4. COINS

Because of overland and sea trade, the people of South Arabia, to be sure, came in contact with coins very early on,[86] yet an exact date is not known. If it can be assumed that the very first coins were made in the early seventh century B.C. in Lydia,[87] this can be used as a reference. From the outset it should be noted that there are still many gaps in our knowledge of ancient South Arabian coinage. This is in part due to the fact that many coins were used in trade and precise information about their origins are lacking. As Dembski[88] has said, even a single new find could fundamentally change the entire picture we have in this field.

Coins were probably first struck in South Arabia—in the Sabaean kingdom—in the fourth[89] or third century B.C.[90] The first coins were imitations of Attic silver tetradachms of the so-called Old Style that had been struck in Athens between 393 and 322 B.C. These Attic coins had the head of the goddess Athena on the obverse side and the Athenian owl with olive spray, crescent moon, and Greek letters on the reverse.

The fact that imitations of these coins were made can be explained by the well developed long-distance trade. That is to say, the Sabaeans must have been familiar with the original Attic tetradrachms quite a while before they started striking their own coins. Also, these coins had very expressive iconography and reliable weight. The popularity of these coins is apparent by the fact that they were copied, not only in South Arabia, but in Egypt, Palestine, and even Central Asia as well.[91]

A short time later, local coins started appearing with additional letters or monograms using the Sabaic alphabet. Another imitation of the Old Style Attic silver tetradrachm shows a beardless man's head instead of Athena on the obverse, while retaining the owl on the reverse. In another series, again, the beardless male "Arab" head is shown on the obverse side, but instead of the owl on the reverse there is a bearded male head. These were probably local rulers.[92]

These were followed by series imitating, for example, New Style Attic silver tetradrachms (late third century–approx. 85 B.C.). After the unsuccessful Roman military campaign of Aelius Gallus in 25-24 B.C., the obverse side of coins from around the first century A.D.[93] showed an Augustan head instead of the Arab. This was followed by a series[94] showing a king or god on the obverse and a bull's head (bucranium) on the reverse. Next came the "king series" from about 50-200 A.D.[95] This is significant in that the reverse side shows a small head with the king's name as well as the mint name, usually Raydān. Coins were no longer minted in South Arabia after around 300 A.D.[96]

The above descriptions refer to Sabaean and the later Ḥimyar silver coins. Knowledge of coins for the kingdoms of Qatabān, Maʿīn, and Ḥaḍramaut is very limited,[97] though more is known about Qatabānian numismatics than the others.[98] From the legend we even know the site of the mint: Ḥarib. According to Doe[99] this was presumably the Royal Palace at Hajar bin-Ḥumeid in Beiḥān (Qatabān), which was also called Ḥarib. The coins described thus far were all made of silver. Were gold and bronze coins also minted? Doe[100] reported that gold coins were rare in South Arabia; this is attested to by Irvine[101] and Hill.[102] Dembski,[103] on the other hand, has said that far more gold coins were minted than the two examples—both in the British Museum—would have us presume. He said that the gold coins were used in long-distance trade and melted down at their destination.

Bronze coins have been confirmed, especially from Ḥaḍramaut. Excavations in Shabwa[104] and the Soviet-Yemenite expeditions in Qanaʾ and Raybūn,[105] as well as the hoard found at Hureihār (near

Raybūn)[106] and in Khōr Rōrī[107] have yielded a large number of bronze coins. This has made it possible to draw up a chronology for bronze Ḥaḍramitic coins. A group of these coins, mostly from Shabwa, have the inscription Shaqir (SQR), that is, the name of the Royal Palace in ancient Shabwa. Only very few bronze coins are known from the other ancient South Arabian kingdoms.[108]

In conclusion, we have been able to gain some insight into ancient South Arabian coinage with respect to, in particular, Saba' and its successor state Ḥimyar, and Ḥaḍramaut. Greece—that is, Athens—provided the initial prototype for the design of the coins. Local strikings later developed to a certain extent, showing some characteristics of their own. Scholarly opinions diverge on the role played by coins in the ancient South Arabian economy. Whereas Doe[109] and Irvine[110] assume that coins were used mainly for external trade and not for internal and domestic transactions, Sedov-Aydarus[111] and Dembski,[112] as well as this author support the notion that silver and bronze coins were hardly used for long-distance trade, most of them serving internal South Arabian trade.

5. POTTERY

The same is true for pottery as for coins: While archaeologists have uncovered a large number of sherds and even intact vessels at excavations, one certainly cannot speak of a systematic classification, typology, or identification of different "ceramic stylistic schools" or centers.[113] This is demonstrated by the fact that the excellent *Jemen Katalog* does not even have a chapter devoted specifically to pottery. We are still miles from achieving the level of knowledge gathered on ceramics in, for instance, Mesopotamia or Iran.

There have nevertheless been attempts in the direction of collecting a corpus of ancient South Arabian pottery, starting with the excavation by Gertrude Caton-Thompson[114] from late 1937 to March 1938 at Ḥureiḍa (Ḥaḍramaut). This was followed by the excavation at Hajar bin Ḥumeid[115] near Timnaʿ (Qatabān) in 1950-51, the French expeditions to Shabwa[116] starting in 1974, the American excavations in Wadi al-Jūbah (between Mārib and Timnaʿ) from 1982 on,[117] and the Soviet-Yemenite missions in Qanaʾ starting in 1985,[118] to name only the most significant ones. These projects have contributed to our insight into developments that ceramics in ancient South Arabia have experienced since around the tenth-ninth centuries B.C. A comparison of ceramics found at the U.S. excavations at Hajar bin Ḥumeid and more recently in Wadi al-Jūbah—they are less than 38 miles apart—have been especially helpful in providing fundamental information.

It can generally be said of South Arabian pottery that the pieces are very simple, in fact primitive. This becomes obvious in comparison with objects from other areas of the Middle East. Neither the methods of production nor the quality of South Arabian ceramics can compete with other ancient Middle Eastern production.[119] It is irrelevant whether or not Van Beek was correct in claiming that styles remained simple because there was little demand for ceramics, as other materials were available for vessels, such as stone (alabaster), skins, or basketry.[120] The same is true for the statement he made in 1969 that there was generally very little pottery at all in South Arabia. Subsequent excavations have since served to modify this view.

I cannot unequivocally accept Van Beek's standpoint that ancient South Arabian ceramics were "principally or perhaps entirely" handmade and that the potter's wheel was not used in pre-Islamic Arabia. This opinion is shared by Doe[121] and Toplyn. The latter has indicated in this context that the wheel as an indispensable means of transportation was lacking in South Arabia. He explained this as being due to the fact that the camel was less expensive and more efficient.

Even if ceramics from Hajar bin Ḥumeid and Wadi al-Jūbah were produced entirely by hand, there are definitely examples of other methods as well. L. Badre[122] said that ceramics from levels I to V in Shabwa were "largely handmade." C. Rathjens[123] determined that the vessels found at his excavation site in Ḥuqqa were "exclusively formed using the wheel." F. P. Albright[124] has said more or less the same about pottery from Sumhuram: "A few pieces were made by hand, but most of it on the wheel." Finally, more recent Russian investigations at Biʾr Ḥamad in the western part of Wadi Ḥaḍramaut report of thirty-five sherds found on the surface, twenty-four of which were "wheelmade."[125] This site is dated in the last quarter of the second millennium to the late first millennium B.C. Regarding the forms of domestic pottery, the inventory found at Hajar bin Ḥumeid is similar to that found at Wadi al-Jūbah. Standard vessels are jugs, dishes, and bowls of all sizes. In terms of decorative styles there were fourteen different categories determined for the ceramics found at Hajar ar-Rayḥānī, one of the main sites in Wadi al-Jūbah,[126] though scratched or raised dot patterns were most common. Similar results were found for pottery from Hajar bin Ḥumeid.

There was a conspicuous share of "foreign" pottery at some sites, although overland and sea trade can easily explain its occurrence. For example, excavations at Qanaʾ showed that up to 80% of ceramic goods were imported,[127] whereby the amphora design was especially common. In Timnaʿ[128] and Shabwa[129] as well, a large amount of imported ceramics were found. The places of provenance of this pottery ranged from Italy and Greece to Africa and the Middle East.

NOTES

I. Geography

1. On the various forms of the name, see Israel Epheʿal, *The Ancient Arabs: Nomads on the borders of the fertile crescent 9th-5th centuries B.C.* [1982], 6ff. (see also the review of that work by H. D. Galter in *BiOr* 41 [1989], col. 747ff.); Epheʿal, in *JNES* 35 (1976), 225ff.; and C. Robin, *L'Arabie antique,* 10ff., 71ff.
2. This probably refers to camel riders; see Epheʿal, *Ancient Arabs,* 165.
3. On Assyrian and Biblical evidence, see J. A. Montgomery, *Arabia and the Bible* (1934).
4. Epheʿal, *Ancient Arabs,* 165.
5. Epheʿal, *JNES* 35, 227.
6. On the different chronologies based on South Arabian inscriptions, see ch. 5, sec. 2 in this book.
7. Epheʿal, *JNES* 35, 233ff.
8. Nat. Hist., book VI, xxxii, 142ff.
9. A. Grohmann, *Arabien* (1963), 3ff.; see also the negative review by J. Pirenne in *BiOr* 23 (1966), 3ff.
10. *EI,* vol. 1 (1960), "Djazīrat al-ʿArab," 533ff.
11. *Geographia* V, 17; V, 19; VI, 7. On the mention of South Arabia in works by classical authors, see also M. Rodinson (and other authors), in Joseph Chelhod, ed., *L'Arabie du Sud: Histoire et civilisation, le peuple yemenite et ses rácines,* tome 1 (1984), 55ff.; and H. I. Macadam, in T. Fahd, ed., *L'Arabie préislamique,* 289ff.
12. On this subject, see also ch. 7 below: "The Economy of South Arabia."
13. Relevant literature refers to various different geographical divisions of northern Yemen; see E. Wohlfahrt, *Die Arabische Halbinsel, Länder zwischen Rotem Meer und Persischem Golf* (1980), 601ff., esp. 602 note 1.
14. See E. Wohlfahrt, 745ff.
15. On the different names for this desert, see E. Wohlfahrt, 761.
16. According to H. von Wissmann, *Zur Archäologie und antiken Geographie von Südarabien. Hadramaut, Qataban und das Aden-Gebiet in der Antike* (1968), 14.

17. See H. von Wissmann, "Geographische Grundlagen und Frühzeit der Geschichte Südarabiens," in *Saeculum* 4 (1953), 61ff. [70].

II. People

1. On this census, see H. Steffen, *Population Geography of the Yemen Arabic Republic* (1979); on population statistics, see also the publications of the German Federal Statistics Office (Statistisches Bundesamt) in Wiesbaden, on North Yemen (1989) and South Yemen (1987). A publication on unified Yemen is in preparation; see also Wohlfahrt, *Arabische Halbinsel,* 974.
2. See Steffen, I/60.
3. Figures have been taken from the German Federal Statistics Office.
4. See *Jemen-Report* 26, no. 2 (1995), 27.
5. See p. 122.
6. The percentage in Saudi Arabia is estimated at 15-25%; see Wohlfahrt, 122 note 1; in the former North Yemen, it was roughly 5%; see H. Dequin, *Arabische Republik Jemen* (1976), 6.
7. Von Wissmann in *Saeculum* 4 (1953), 70.
8. For example, see H. von Wissmann and Maria Höfner, *Beiträge* (1952), 282 (64) and 294 (76), and F. Hommel, *Ethnologie und Geographie des Alten Orients* (1926), 658, esp. note 3, where some figures from inscriptions are listed. There, Karibʾīl Watār, ruler of Sabaʾ, is said to have killed 16,000 people during a campaign against the ʾAusān kingdom, and to have taken 40,000 people prisoner. Another inscription referred to as many as 45,000 casualties and 63,000 prisoners in a war against Najrān.
9. See U. Brunner, "Die Erforschung der antiken Oase von Marib mit Hilfe geomorphologischer Untersuchungsmethoden," *ABADY* 2 (1983), 116.
10. *PSAS* 1 (1970), 26ff.; 5 (1975), 7 note 1; see also A. H. al-Sheiba, *ABADY* 4 (1988), 1ff.
11. See U. Brunner, 105-6, 122; W. W. Müller, *al-Yaman* calendar, reverse of "February," refers to 9600 hectares (roughly 24,000 acres). According to J. Hehmeier, *ABADY* 5 (1990), 81-82, the total amount of irrigated cultivated land area is 7170 hectares (over 17,700 acres).
12. *Arabien*, 142, which cites E. Glaser; W. W. Müller, *EI* 6 (1990), 559ff. lists 110 hectares (272 acres); B. Doe, *Monuments of South Arabia*, 121,

which cites von Wissmann, who in turn cited from Glaser's journal: 70 hectares (about 173 acres).

13. See Brunner, 105, who cited R. Schoch, *Geographica Helvetica* 33, no. 3 (1978), 126.

14. Brunner's (p. 106) reference to a population figure of the same magnitude in an essay by H. Dequin, *Orient* 9, no. 5 (1968), 164ff., 166, is only partly correct. Dequin assumed an area of only about 7400 acres (3000 ha); he referred to 30,000 people, but then came to the conclusion that a population figure of 100,000 could easily be reached by including additional means of subsistence (caravans, livestock breeding). On this, see the article by G.W. Van Beek in *BASOR* 248 (1982), 61ff. on the population figures for Marīb. In "Marīb," *EI* 6 (1990), 563, W. W. Müller referred to a minimum of 30,000 and a maximum of 50,000 inhabitants.

15. C. Rathjens (Sr.) and C. Rathjens (Jr.) and others, in *Beiträge zur Klimakunde Südwest-Arabiens, Deutscher Wetterdienst, Seewetteramt, Einzelveröffentlichungen* [articles on the climate of southwestern Arabia, the German Weather Service, and meteorological service; individual publications] 11 (1956), 34; also in *Sabaeica, Bericht über die archäologischen Ergebnisse seiner zweiten, dritten und vierten Reise nach Südarabien*, part II (1955), 24.

16. Sammlung Eduard Glaser III, "Zur Geschichte und Landeskunde von Alt-Südarabien," *ÖAkWS* 246 (1964), 371-72.

17. See ibid., map on pp. 294-95.

18. The size of Marīb as listed in the references ranges from 173 to 282 acres (see note 12, above). Even assuming a size of 173 acres, Marīb is much larger than all the other cities in Old South Arabia. Timnaʿ, the second largest city, is about 52-59 acres, according to Brian Doe, *Monuments of South Arabia*, 129 (the figure is incorrectly converted to 37 ha.); or 59 acres (24 ha), according to H. von Wissmann, *Le Muséon* 75 (1962), 193; the von Wissmann essay also mentions the sizes of other towns.

19. See H. von Wissmann, "Die Geschichte des Sabäerreiches und der Feldzug des Aelius Gallus," in *ANRW* II, 9.1 (1976), 433.

20. Die Erde. *Zeitschrift der Gesellschaft für Erdkunde* 129 (1990), 135ff.

21. See the beginning of this chapter, p. 9.

22. The figures for the Indus civilization have been taken from the essay by G. F. Dales in the catalogue *Vergessene Städte am Indus* (1987), 137ff.

23. See ch. 5, sec. 1, "The prehistoric period."

24. As general references for the Arabian region as a whole, see *Proceedings*

of the Seminar for Arabian Studies and the journal *Arabian Archaeology and Epigraphy*.

25. The South Yemenite journal *Raydan* is a good reference on excavations in the former South Yemen, among other things. The bibliography and excavation reports for South Arabia in W. W. Müller's *AfO* should be considered, most recently *AfO* 44-45 (1997-98), 595ff. See also the Italian journal *Yemen Studi archeologici, storici e filologici sull'Arabia meridionale*, starting in 1992. In 1996, the first two issues of the periodical *Abiel* appeared (ed. D. T. Potts and M. L. A. Macdonald); they deal with research throughout the entire Arabian peninsula.

26. The journal *Oman Studies* is significant regarding research in Oman.

27. For Saudi Arabia, the journal *Atlal*.

28. For the United Arab Emirates, *Archaeology in the United Arab Emirates*.

29. *Arabien*, 9ff.

30. In *Handbuch der geographischen Wissenschaften*, ed. F. Klute, 5 (1937), part 4, "Arabian," 178ff., 200ff. On the early history of Arabia and the emergence of the Sabaean kingdom, see *Die Geschichte von Saba'*, part I, *Sammlung Eduard Glaser* 13, *ÖAkWS* 301, treatise 5 (1975), 8ff.; see also A. E. Knauf, *PSAS* 18 (1988), 39ff.

31. *Die Geschichte von Saba'*, part II. "Das Grossreich der Sabäer bis zu seinem Ende im frühen 9. Jh. v. Chr.," *ÖAkWS* 402 (1982), 13ff.; similar, albeit much more concise, is Müller, *Jemen-Katalog*, Munich (1987), 50.

32. According to D. T. Potts, *PSAS* 17 (1984), 87ff. In Müller's opinion, the Hasaitic name "Hajar" is based on the Greek name "Gerrha"; see von Wissmann, Die Geschichte von Saba', part II, 29 note 21a.

33. *Jemen-Katalog*, 109-10.

34. See *Die Geschichte von Saba'*, part I, 8, and II, 21ff.

35. See D. T. Potts, *The Arabian Gulf in Antiquity*, 1: "From Prehistory to the fall of the Achaemenid Empire" (1990), 81-82, 129-30.

36. *Die Geschichte von Saba'*, part I, 8ff.

37. Named for the Gonds, who live in the interior of the northern half of the Deccan. See the short yet important essay by Hella Pöch, "Über die äthiopide und die gondide Rasse und ihre Verbreitung" in *Anthropologischer Anzeiger* 21 (1957), 147ff.

38. Their name comes from their skin color: Greek *aithiops* means, approximately, sunburned.

39. *Arabien*, 12.

40. Most informative are still the works by Grohmann and von Wissmann, and the short essay by Hella Pöch. See also *Rassengeschichte der Menschheit* 14, *Asien IV: Südwestasien*, ed. W. Bernhard (1993), 169ff.

III. Languages and Writing

1. For further literature on the subject of this section, see A. F. L. Beeston, "Vorislamische Inschriften und vorislamische Sprachen des Jemen," in *Jemen Katalog,* Munich (1987), 102ff., though it is very specific. Also, in the same catalogue, see G. Garbini, "Semitische und indoeuropäische Sprachen," 107ff., and, albeit somewhat outdated, the instructive section by Maria Höfner, "Das Südarabische der Inschriften und lebenden Mundarten," in *Handbuch der Orientalistik,* vol. 3: "Semitistik," Leiden (1954), 314ff.; see also C. Robin, in *L'Arabie antique,* 17ff., 89ff.; W. W. Müller, *Die altsüdarabische Schrift. Ein interdisziplinäres Handbuch internationaler Forschung,* ed. H. Günther and D. Ludwig, vol. 1 of 2 (1994), 307ff.; and F. Bron, *Vienna Catalogue,* 77ff.

2. On this, see G. Garbini, ibid.

3. See Höfner, *Handbuch*, 317.

4. See J. Ryckmans, *PSAS* 5 (1975), 61.

5. An example can be found on the *al-Yaman* calendar (1991), reverse side of "June."

6. See A. F. L. Beeston, *Jemen Katalog,* and J. Ryckmans, *al-Yaman* calendar (1991), reverse side of "November"; C. Robin in *L'Arabie antique,* 132-33, and, above all, J. Ryckmans, W. W. Müller, Y. Abdallah, *Textes du Jemen antique. Inscrits du bois* (1994); and more recently, Y. M. Abdallah and I. Gajda, *Vienna Catalogue,* 192ff.

7. M. Höfner, *Handbuch,* 320, still spoke of dialects.

8. *PSAS* 17 (1987), 13-14 and in *Jemen Katalog,* 102ff.

9. First of all, A. F. L. Beeston, M. A. Ghul, W. W. Müller, J. Ryckmans, *Sabaic Dictionary (English-French-Arabic)* (see the extensive review by N. Nebes in *BiOr* 42 [1985], col. 23ff.); see also J. C. Biella, *Dictionary of Old South Arabic. Sabaean Dialect* (and the review by N. Nebes in *BiOr* 41 [1984], col. 501ff.).

10. Northern semitic includes, among others, the Ugarit, Phoenician, and Proto-Canaanite alphabets. Southern semitic includes Old South Arabic,

Proto-Arabic, and a few other alphabets.

11. Literature on this debate is very elaborate and usually only makes sense to specialists in the field. In my opinion, the book best suited to provide information on the problems is M. Dietrich and O. Loretz, *Die Keilalphabete. Die phönizisch-kanaanäischen und alt-arabischen Alphabete in Ugarit, Abhandlungen zur Literatur Alt-Syrien-Palästinas (ALASP),* vol. 1 (1988). It discusses the various different opinions appearing in literature and takes a stand. An abridged edition of this work, including a supplement by the two authors, can be found in *Ugarit-Forschungen* 21 (1989), 101ff.

12. See *La Grèce et Saba* (1955), 102ff.; and "Überblick über die Lehrmeinungen zur altsüdarabischen Chronologie," *Jemen Katalog,* Munich (1987), 122ff.

13. See *Harvard Theological Studies* 12 (1969), 15.

14. See, for instance, E. A. Knauf, *PSAS* 19 (1989), 79ff. [83].

15. See *Le Muséon* 100 (1987), 243ff.; *al-Yaman* calendar (1991), reverse side of "March"; see also C. Robin in *L'Arabie antique,* 127ff.

16. Opinions diverge considerably on the significance and dating of this clay tablet; see M. Dietrich and D. Loretz, *Die Keilalphabete,* 277ff.; J. Ryckmans, *PSAS* 18 (1988), 123ff.; and, finally, B. Sass, *Ugarit-Forschungen* 23 (1991), 315ff.

17. See *Bulletin des Séances de L'Academie Royale des Sciences d'Outre-Mer* (Louvain-la-Neuve) 32 (1986), 311ff; and 34 (1988), 219ff.; see also *PSAS* 18 (1988), 123ff.

IV. Exploration History

1. A good, recent summary can be found in *L'Arabie du Sud, histoire et civilisation,* tome 1, 91ff., 111ff.; see also G. Rohner and H. R. von Rohr, *Yemen. Land am "Tor der Tränen"* (1979), 36ff.; J. Pirenne, *A la découverte de l'Arabie—cinq siècles de science et d'aventure* (1985); F. Hommel, *Ethnologie und Geographie des Alten Orients, Handbuch der Altertumswissenschaft,* sec. 3, part 1, vol. 1 (1926), 522ff.; A. Grohmann, *Arabien,* 95ff. Particularly the last two works include references to the publications of researchers named in the following.

2. See Grohmann, *Arabien,* 101 note 1.

3. There is much disagreement as to how the name should be pronounced. See J. Pirenne, *Oman Studies* 1 (1975), 81ff., and A. F. L. Beeston, *Oman*

Studies 2 (1976), 39ff.

4. A precursor to this book appeared in 1970 under the title *Southern Arabia.*

5. See W. Radt, *Archäologischer Anzeiger* 1971, 235ff.

6. See Pirenne, *Raydan* 1 (1978), 125ff., J.-F. Breton, R. Audouin, and J. Seigne, *Raydan* 4 (1981), 163ff.; J.-F. Breton, *Jemen Katalog,* 116ff. A summary of all the excavation findings can be found in *Syria* 68 (1991), 1-431.

7. See J.-F. Breton, *Raydan* 2 (1979), 185ff.

8. See C. Robin, *CRAI* (1981), 315ff.; C. Robin and J. Ryckmans, *Raydan* 3 (1980), 113ff.

9. See H. Hauptmann, *Yemen Arab Republic, Archaeological Research, Restricted Technical Report,* Serial no. FMR/CC/CH/78/106 (PP), Paris 1978.

10. Eight comprehensive volumes have been published since 1982 in the institute series *Archäologische Berichte aus dem Yemen.*

11. See the essays by G. M. Bulgarelli, F. G. Fedele, and A. de Maigret in *Jemen Katalog,* 33ff. These research projects will be discussed in greater detail in the next chapter, "The History of South Arabia" in sec. 1: The prehistoric period.

V. History

1. See *Geographical Journal* 93 (1939), 18ff.; *Proceedings of the Prehistoric Society* 19 (1953), 189ff.

2. See G. L. Harding, *Archaeology in the Aden Protectorates* (1964).

3. See G. W. Van Beek, G. H. Cole, and A. Jamme, *The Smithsonian Report* (1963), 521ff.

4. See *Southern Arabia,* 134-35, see also 227; J. Chelhod, *L'Arabie du Sud,* tome 1, 27; According to the latter, the finds at Jabal Tala were made by a Russian mission, under the leadership of S. Chirinski, in 1972. But since Doe had already reported on the objects in his book published in 1970, there must be two different sites in the same area.

5. Citing Doe, G. M. Bulgarelli, *Jemen Katalog,* 34, gives the following dates: 400,000-200,000 years ago, while Chelhod speaks of 500,000-200,000 years ago, citing Chirinski.

6. See Bulgarelli, *Jemen Katalog,* 33-34; and *East and West* 33 (1983), 343.

7. See Garbini in *AION* 30 (1979), 400ff., 537ff.; see also Bulgarelli, *Jemen Katalog*, 33-34; R. Bayle des Hermens, in *L'Arabie du Sud,* tome 1, 186.

8. See R. Bayle des Hermens, *L'Anthropologie* 80 (1976), 5ff.; 84 (1980), 563ff.; *L'Arabie du Sud,* tome 1, 185ff.; see also M. L. Inizan, *Raydan* 5 (1988), 71, on a survey in the Shabwa region.

9. On rock drawings, see also M. Jung, *East and West* 41 (1991), 47ff., and *AION* 49 (1989), 271ff.; 50 (1990), 41ff.; and *PSAS* 24 (1994), 135ff.

10. One of the most significant formations is located near the Hodeida-Taizz route. It is known as "al-Hajar al-Ghaimah" ("the standing stones"); see H. Peters, *Jemen Report* 5 (1974), 12ff.; but he was not the first visitor there. Earlier, G. Benardelli and A.E. Parrinello had already described this site; see *AION* 30 (1970), 117ff. See more recently, B. Vogt, *Vienna Catalogue,* 123ff [124]. See also the essay by W. Dostal, "Zur Megalithfrage in Südarabien," Festschrift Werner Caskel, ed. E. Gräf (1968), 53ff.

11. The site is located about 40-50 km southeast of Sanaa; see A. de Maigret, *Raydan* 4 (1981), 197-98; G.M. Bulgarelli, *East and West* 33 (1983), 342-43; *Jemen Katalog,* 33.

12. See Bulgarelli, ibid.

13. See the articles by Bulgarelli, F. G. Gedele, and de Maigret in *Jemen Katalog,* 33ff.; other sources are also listed there. See also the three above-named authors in *East and West* 35 (1985), 337ff.; de Maigret, *Raydan* 4 (1981), 194ff., and de Maigret, et al, *Paléorient* 15/1 (1989), 239ff. Regarding neolithic finds in the Ramlat Ṣayhad desert, see F. di Mario, *AION* 49 (1989), 109ff.; and, recently, M. L. Inizan, *Vienna Catalogue,* 103ff.

14. See M. R. Toplyn, *The Wadi al-Jubah Archaeological Project,* vol. 1: Site Reconnaissance in North Jemen (1982), American Foundation for the Study of Man; J. A. Blakely, J. A. Sauer, and M. R. Toplyn, vol. 2 (1985); W. D. Glanzman, A. O. Ghaleb, et al., vol. 3 (1987); W. C. Overstreet, M. J. Grolier, M. R. Toplyn, et al., vol. 4; J.A. Blakely and J. A. Sauer, *Expedition* 27 (1985), 2ff.; also J. A. Blakely and J. A. Sauer, in: *Araby the Blest,* ed. D. Potts (1988), 91ff. (with a comprehensive bibliography).

15. See Bulgarelli, *Jemen Katalog,* 36.

16. See J.-F. Breton, *Jemen Katalog,* 119.

17. See the sources listed under notes 8 and 13; see also Fedele, *Jemen Katalog,* 35ff.; de Maigret, Bulgarelli, and others, *East and West* 35

(1985), 337ff. Fedele dates this period in the time from around 20,000-2000 B.C.

18. See Brian Doe, *Southern Arabia,* 227; ——, *Monuments of South Arabia,* 36; and, recently, R. Vogt, *Vienna Catalogue,* 111ff.

19. *Southern Arabia,* 227, citing G. Lankester Harding. However, Doe is incorrect in referring to this as belonging to the Ḥaḍramaut geographical area; Habarūt is located in the Mahra region.

20. See Breton, *Jemen Katalog,* 119.

21. See de Maigret, *Jemen Katalog,* 39ff.; ——, *East and West* 34 (1984), 75ff., *East and West* 35 (1985), 352ff.; L. Constantini, *East and West* 34 (1984), 107ff.; Fedele, *East and West* 34, 117ff.; and more recently, de Maigret, "The Bronze Age Culture of Ḫawlan aṭ-Ṭiyāl and al-Hada, Reports and Memoirs," *ISMEO* 24 (1990). In this context the Ṣabir civilization along the coastal plain from the Tihāma to Aden in the second half of the second century B.C. is also interesting and significant; see B. Vogt and A. V. Sedov, *Vienna Catalogue,* 129; also, in ch. 6 of this book, pp. 72-74.

22. See note 14; also, E.A. Knauf, *PSAS* 18 (1988), 39ff. [46ff.].

23. For the various countries, refer especially to the previously mentioned journals (see notes 24-28 in ch. 2, "The People").

24. The American excavations in Hajar bin Ḥumeid (the area of Beiḥān, the former kingdom of Qatabān) yielded only two C-14 datings: 852-51 B.C. ± 160 and 740 B.C. ± 100. First of all, two dates are far too few, and secondly, the possible deviations of 160 and 100 are far too high. On this, see G. Van Beek, *Hajar Bin Humeid, Investigations at a Pre-Islamic Site in South Arabia,* Publ. of the American Foundation for the Study of Man (1969), 355ff.; J. Ryckmans, review of the book by Van Beek in *BiOr* 29 (1972), 237, and von Wissmann, *ANRW* II/9.1 (1976), 322.

25. On the role of paleography, see J. Ryckmans, *al-Yaman* calendar (1991), reverse side of "November."

26. See J. Ryckmans, "La Chronologie sud-arabe du premier siècle avant notre ère." *BiOr* 10 (1953), 205ff.; see also J. Pirenne, *BiOr* 26 (1969), 303ff., which includes a list of the other articles that appeared in *BiOr.* Regarding articles that appeared after 1969, see, for example, E.G. Loundine (Lundin), *BiOr* 35 (1978), 384ff., and *BiOr* 37 (1980), 363ff., and Pirenne, *BiOr* 41 (1984), col. 569ff.

27. However, the three chronologies in Mesopotamian archaeology have a totally different basis.

28. These names have been taken from Pirenne, *Jemen Katalog,* 122. This catalogue is, incidentally, the prime example of the disagreement among scholars: Pirenne (see p. 122ff.) supports the "Short Chronology," as does Breton (120). W.W. Müller (50ff.) and J. Schmidt (84), on the other hand, base their findings on the "Long Chronology."

29. See *Skizze der Geschichte und Geographie Arabiens (bis Muhammad)* II (1890), 18.

30. In *Handbuch der altarabischen Altertumskunde*, 57ff. [85].

31. Gl. 1703 means inscription number 1703 of the inscriptions found and collected by E. Glaser and his team.

32. "Mukarrib" was initially translated as "priest king," according to Hommel in the *Handbuch der altarabischen Altertumskunde,* ed. D. Nielsen, p. 77. On the expression "mukarrib," see also J. Ryckmans, *L'Institution Monarchique,* 51ff., 97ff., and *PSAS* 2 (1971), 24ff. It should be kept in mind, however, that the areas of competence of these mukarribs in Saba' were primarily secular in nature, such as waging wars and having irrigation systems built (see Beeston, *PSAS* 7 [1977], 5ff.). Jamme (*BiOr* 12 [1953], 219ff. [220]) wrote that "mukarrib" might be derived from the Arabic word "karaba," which means something like "weaving a rope" or "strengthening connections." This interpretation would apply far better to the early Sabaean period, when the unification of the tribes was a major concern. This opinion was adopted by Pirenne (*Paléographie,* 144ff.). One could speak of the "unifier of the land." In a similar vein, see C. Robin, *Jemen Katalog,* 77, and Beeston, *EI* 8 (1995), 664.

33. See Pirenne, *La Grèce et Saba,* 89ff. [95ff.]. Only H. Philby continued to support this "Long Chronology"; see *Le Muséon* 63 (1950), 229ff. [235ff.].

34. In addition to von Wissmann in, for example, *Zur Archäologie und antiken Geographie von Südarabien* (1968), 6; *ANRW* II/9.1 (1976), 320ff., other examples that could be mentioned are: A. Grohmann, *Arabien,* 24 (here, the beginning of the Mukarrib Period is set as early as the 9th century B.C. or possible even earlier); Müller, *Jemen Katalog,* 50. This dating is also assumed by the series published by the German Archaeological Institute in Sanaa.

35. See *Handbuch,* 85.

36. *Jemen Katalog,* 128.

37. See "Sabaean Inscriptions from Maḥram Bilqîs (Mârib)," *Publications of the American Foundation for the Study of Man* 3 (1962), 389.

38. See *Akten des 24. Internationalen Orientalisten-Kongresses in München 1957* (Annals of the 24th International Orientalist Congress in Munich 1957) (1959), 153ff.

39. See *L'Institution Monarchique,* 51, 274.

40. See *JEOL* 15 (1957-58), 239ff. [241]; *La chronologie des rois de Saba et Dū-Raydān* (1964), 1; *BiOr* 21 (1964), 376ff.

41. See Robin, *L'Arabie antique,* 25ff.

42. See "Die Eponymenliste von Saba (aus dem Stamme Ḫalīl)", *Sammlung Eduard Glaser* 5, *ÖAkWS* 248, 1 (1965), 96.

43. In *BSOAS* 16 (1954), 37ff. [44], and later in *EI* 8 (1995), 663, he dated the oldest group of Sabaean inscriptions (aside from a few earlier ones) in the eighth century B.C.

44. Above all, in *La Grèce et Saba;* in addition, she expressed her opinion in numerous reviews in *BiOr* (see note 26). See *Jemen Katalog,* 122ff., for a relatively recent example.

45. *Jemen Katalog,* 124-26.

46. *BiOr* 16 (1959), 76ff.; see also J. Ryckmans's article on the role and aim of paleography in *L'Arabie antique,* 25ff.

47. See p. 21.

48. See Dietrich and Loretz, *Keilalphabete,* 57ff. [61]. The differing opinions are presented here.

49. *BiOr* 19 (1962), 206.

50. *PSAS* 18 (1988), 123ff. [125].

51. For example, see M. Rodinson in "L'écriture et la psychologie des peuples," *Centre internationale de Synthèse,* 22nd Semaine de Synthèse, Paris (1963), 131ff.; I. J. Gelb, *A Study of Writing,* 2nd printing (1963), x-xi, 133; Robin, in *Chelhod L'Arabie du Sud,* tome 1, 206ff., did not rule out a correction based on more recent archaeological finds. This was then made about twenty years later, see p. 48.

52. *BASOR* 143 (1956), 10, as well as Beeston, *BSOAS* 16 (1954), 42-43 and Pirenne, *La Gréce et Saba,* 98ff.

53. This is the "commonly" held view; see, for example, J. Ryckmans, *L'Institution Monarchique,* 59, 96; H. von Wissmann, *ANRW* II/9.1, 364. The number "14" for the generations of rulers has been taken from Beeston, *BiOr* 16 (1959), 77. In *BSOAS* 16 (1954), 44, he speaks of "probably" 15 mukarribs. Pirenne, *La Grèce et Saba,* 124, refers to the number 22.

54. According to, among others, *Paléographie,* 116ff.

55. *BiOr* 16 (1959), 78.

56. *Paléographie,* 211ff.

57. This is a Minaean inscription, which is part of the "Répertoire d'Epigraphie sémitique" (RES), a collection founded in the year 1900 in Paris.

58. Mentioned as early as W. M. Müller, *Mitt. der Vorderasiatischen Gesellschaft* 3 (1898), 3, 41; see also W. W. Tarn, *Journal of Egyptian Archaeology* 15 (1929), 9ff. [17]; F. V. Winnett, *BASOR* 73 (1939), 3ff. [8]; W. F. Albright, *BASOR* 119 (1950), 5ff. [15] and *BASOR* 129 (1953), 20ff. [22]; von Wissmann, *ANRW* II/9.1, 363, 383-84; W. W. Müller, *Jemen Katalog,* 51. J. Ryckmans initiallly supported the notion that these referred to one and the same event (*L'Institution Monarchique,* 267), though later, in *JEOL* 15 (1957-58), 243, he referred to the year 198 B.C.; in 1961 he changed his opinion to concur with Pirenne's, *Recueil de Travaux d'Histoire et de Phil.,* Université de Louvain, 4th ser., fasc. 24 (1961), 51ff. [57].

59. See *ANRW* II/9.1, 384, note 156.

60. On the story of the discovery of these inscriptions, see A. G. Lundin, "Die Eponymenliste von Saba (aus dem Stamme Ḫalīl)," *Sammlung Eduard Glaser* 5, *ÖAkWS* 248, 1 (1965), 9ff.

61. See Pirenne, *BiOr* 41 (1984), col. 569ff. [p. 576ff.]; here, once again, is the never-ending paleographic debate between Pirenne and von Wissmann, which can be grasped and understood by only very few specialists.

62. See *Jemen Katalog,* 124 and plate 3 (p. 127).

63. See R. Göbl, *Antike Numismatik* 1 (1978), 59, where Göbl declares that "the owl type supposedly did not appear until the late sixth century." Göbl seems to support an earlier date; C. M. Kraay, *Archaic and Classical Coins* (1976), 60ff.: in the final quarter of the seventh century B.C.

64. See R. Göbl, 142ff.; and E. Ebeling, "Geld" in *Reallexikon der Assyriologie* 3 (1971), 198.

65. See *La Grèce et Saba,* 111-12, 142; *Jemen Katalog,* 124.

66. In *Archaeological Discoveries in South Arabia,* Publ. of the American Foundation for the Study of Man, ed. R. LeBaron Bowen Jr. and F.P. Albright, vol. 2 (1958), 287ff.

67. In *ABADY* 4 (1988), 63ff.; see also M. N. van Loon, *Urartian Art, its distinctive traits in the light of new excavations* (1966), 52.

68. *La Grèce et Saba*, 112, 142; *Paléographie*, 142; and more recently, in *L'Arabie préislamique*, 256.

69. In *ABADY* 4 (1988), plate, 77.

70. This evidently greatly impressed Beeston in terms of chronology in his discussion of Pirenne's book *La Grèce et Saba;* see *BiOr* 17 91960), 199.

71. *L Grèce et Saba*, 142.

72. *Paléographie*, 142.

73. See C. Nylander, *Iranica Antiqua* 6 (1966), 130ff. [132ff.].

74. According to Pirenne in *La Grèce et Saba*, 154ff.; *Jemen Katalog*, 124.

75. In *Syria* 38 (1961), 296.

76. See *Baghdader Mitteilungen* 10 (1979), 155. The cited passed has been translated from the original German.

77. In *L'Arabie préislamique*, 281ff.; see also the discussion on finds in the Temple of ʾAwwām in Mārib in Almut Hauptmann–von Gladiss, *Baghdader Mitteilungen* 10 (1979), 146-47, note 7.

78. See, for example, the bronze statuette in *Jemen Katalog*, 91.

79. Hauptmann–von Gladiss, op. cit., 157.

80. In *L'Arabie préislamique*, 271ff.

81. Hauptmann–von Gladiss, op. cit., 149-50, plate 28, 1-4.

82. See *Paléographie*, 122.

83. See "Die Königin von Saba," ed. W. Daum (1988), 36.

84. See the excavation publication by Gus W. Van Beek, with articles by Jamme and others: *Hajar bin Humeid* (1969); —— in *BASOR* 143 (1956), 6ff.; W.F. Albright, 9ff.; a positive evaluation by von Wissmann, *ANRW* II/9.1 (1976), 321-22, 329, 369; —— in *Die Geschichte von Sabaʾ*, vol. 2 (1982), 63ff.

85. See *Le Royaume Sud-Arabe de Qataban* (1961), 38-39; *Syria* 51 (1974), 137ff.; *Revue Archéologique* 1973, 323ff.

86. *BiOr* 29 (1972), 236-37; see also P. Parr in *Studies*, 49.

87. See Van Beek, *Hajar bin Humeid*, 356ff.

88. See *Atlal* 7 (1986), 31. At the same time Zarins feels that the Zubayda ceramics (see note 89) could provide further information.

89. *Atlal* 4 (1980), 116. For the C-14 data, see Zarins, note 88.

90. *ANRW* II, 9.1, 322.

91. For both, see *BASOR* 143 (1956), 6, 10.

92. *BiOr* 29 (1972), 237.

93. See note 14 above, with references listed; see esp. vol. 3, 208.

94. See *Expedition* 27 (1985), 8; *Araby the Blest,* ed. D. Potts (1988), 100.

95. In *Die Königin von Saba,* ed. W. Daum (1988), 36ff. [38-39]; and more recently, *The Sabaean Archaeological Complex in the Wadi Yala. A Preliminary Report. Reports and Memoirs (ISMEO)* 21 (1988), and C. Robin *CRAI* (1989), 278ff.

96. See, in *Reports and Memoirs (ISMEO)* 21 (1988), 19, 21ff.; and *Yemen Studi archeologici, storici e filologici sull'Arabia meridionale* 1 (1992), 79ff. [87ff.].

97. See L. Badre, *Syria* 68 (1991), 232ff.

98. See Brunner, *ABADY* 2 (1983), 66, 74, 108ff.

99. See *ABADY* 6 (1993), 92ff.; noteworthy is also the introductory comments by the editor J. Schmidt, according to which, despite all findings up to now, the final word has not yet been spoken; see also M. Schaloske, *ABADY* 7 (1995), 164, 170, who drew similar conclusions to Wagner's.

100. Through the review of this book by Müller in *BiOr* 51 (1994), 468ff.

101. It appeared as *Revue du Monde Musulman et de la Méditerranée* 61 (1991-93); see also Robin, *Vienna Catalogue,* 71ff.

102. See *L'Arabie antique,* 50ff., 128ff.

103. See note 95 in this chapter.

104. See A. V. Sedov, in *Ancient and Mediaeval Monuments of Civilization of Southern Arabia* (1988), 61ff. For inscriptions, see S. A. Frantsouzoff, *PSAS* 25 (1995), 15ff. Recently, see A. V. Sedov and P. Griaznevich, eds., *Raybūn Settlement (1983-1987 excavations). Preliminary Reports of the Soviet-Yemeni Complex Expedition,* vol. 2 (Moscow, 1996) [in Russian].

105. See Robin, *L'Arabie antique,* 128ff.; and *EI* 9 (1995), 90ff.

106. See Robin, ibid., 51.

107. K. A. Kitchen, *The World of Ancient Arabia Series, Documentation for Ancient Arabia (DAA),* part 1: "Chronological Framework and Historical Sources," (Liverpool 1994). See the review by W. W. Müller,

OLZ 92 (1997), col. 549; further, A. Sims, *AfO* 44/45 (1997/98), 441ff. The date 1200 B.C. is mentioned on p. 132 and elsewhere. I gained access to this very detailled work only shortly before this book was completed, and was not able to consider it extensively. See also A. Avanzini in *Quaderni di Studi Arabi* 11 (1993), 7ff.: "Long Chronology," and G. Garbini, in the same journal, 19ff.: "Short Chronology."

108. On the term "capital," see Beeston, *PSAS* 1 (1970), 26ff.; *PSAS* 5 (1975), 7, note 1. On Saba' in general see also the article by Beeston, "Saba'," *EI* 8 (1994), 663ff; on Mārib see Müller, *EI* 6 (1991), 559ff.

109. See Brunner, *ABADY* 2 (1983), 109-10, possibly even earlier, see this chapter above, note 99 and p. 48.

110. Müller, *Jemen Katalog,* 53.

111. *ANRW* II/9.1, 362, 415.

112. *Jemen Katalog,* 51.

113. *BASOR* 129 (1953), 20ff.

114. *Jemen Katalog,* 124ff.; in Qatabān, p. 7, 54; however, she sets the beginning around 300 B.C. and the end around 250 A.D.

115. See *L'Institution Monarchique,* 268-69. Later (see here, ch. 5, sec. 2, notes 39-41), he joined Pirenne's "Short Chronology" camp, only to reject it again at a later date.

116. On trade relations, see J. Ryckmans, *JEOL* 15 (1957-58), 242ff.

117. On the geography of 'Ausān, see von Wissmann and Höfner, *Beiträge,* 275ff.; J. Pirenne, *Raydan* 3 (1980), 213ff., and *Raydan* 4 (1981), 205ff.

118. See *Raydan* 3, 238 and *Raydan* 4, 234; Lankester Harding, *Archaeology in the Aden Protectorates,* 1; Doe, *Southern Arabia,* 73 and H. St. John Philby, *Sheba's Daughters* (1939), 346-48 believe it is Hajar an Nāb in the same wadi, but about 6 miles farther west; J.-F. Breton, *Raydan* 6 (1994), 41ff. believes it is Hajar Yahirr (Yahar), further east in Wadi Markha.

119. I was unable to find a date in the relevant literature.

120. *Raydan* 4, 231; however, in *Raydan* 3, 236 she reports the year 400.

121. *L'Institution Monarchique,* 274; Doe, *Southern Arabia,* 73 gives a similar date: 410 B.C.

122. *Beiträge,*288-89.

123. *ANRW* II/9.1, 353 and 333, respectively.

124. *Beiträge,* 69-70.

125. *Syria* 38 (1961), 284ff.; see also *Raydan* 4, 234; and Beeston, *BiOr* 9 (1952), 215; *AfO* 17 (1954-56), 166; J. Ryckmans, *BiOr* 11 (1954), 136.

126. *Jahrbuch für Kleinasiatische Forschung* 1 (1950), 28.

127. See Pirenne, *Raydan* 3 (1980), 234ff.

128. The two forms of the name are by no means absolutely certain. Even among authors of antiquity, the forms Tamna and Kitibaina can be found. On this, see Müller, *Jemen Report* 9 (1975), 14, which offers an overview of the history of Qatabān. See also von Wissmann, *ANRW* II, 9.1, 539. However, the standard work on this kingdom remains Pirenne, *Le Royaume Sud-Arabe de Qataban es sa Datation* (1961). See also Robin, "Qatabān," in *Suppl. au Dictionaire de la Bible,* facs. 50B (1979), 597ff [col.. 598]; Beeston, "Kataban," in *EI* 4 (1978), 746; and Bafaqih, *L'Unification du Yemen antique* (1990), 195ff. More recently, see A. Avanzini, *Vienna Catalogue,* 169ff.

129. Von Wissmann, *ANRW* II, 9.1, 353, dated the inscription at 685 B.C. In Pirenne, *Paléographie,* 118, chart following p. 337, it is dated at 430 B.C.

130. According to, for example, Müller in *Jemen Katalog,* 51; W.F. Albright in *BASOR* 119 (1980), 5ff [11] dates the "entire monarchy of Qatabān" at 400-50 B.C. However, according to Albright, the first mukarribs are documented as early as the sixth century B.C. Pirenne, *Qataban,* 7, dates it at 300 B.C.

131. See Müller, *Jemen Katalog,* 51.

132. See von Wissmann, *ANRW* II, 9.1, 395.

133. *BASOR* 119 (1950), 6 note 4, 13.

134. *ANRW* II, 9.1, 455; Doe, *Southern Arabia,* 72: A.D. 10; Müller, *Jemen Katalog,* 52, dates the destruction of Timnaʿ in the first quarter of the first century A.D. and the end of the Qatabānian kingdom in the second half of the second century.

135. Pirenne, *Qataban,* 7, 29, chart following 232; According to Müller, *Jemen Katalog,* 52, it was the second half of the second century A.D.; according to J. Ryckmans, *La chronologie des rois de Saba et Du Ráydan* (1984), 746, it was the end of the second century or somewhat later; and according to Beeston, *EI* 4 (1978), 746, after the end of the fourth century A.D., at the latest, Qatabān is no longer mentioned in the inscriptions. Kitchen, *The World of Ancient Arabia* series, part I, 37

gives the date as 160 A.D.

136. See Müller, *Jemen Katalog,* 53.

137. See *Southern Arabia,* 100.

138. See *Raydan* 4 (1981), 184; Beeston, "Ḥaḍramaut," *EI* 3 (1979), 51ff.: end of the third century A.D.

139. *Beiträge,* 334-35.

140. On the Ḥimyarites, see von Wissmann, "Ḥimyar, Ancient History," *Le Muséon* 77 (1964), 429ff. The critical review by Beeston should also be taken into account: *PSAS* 5 (1975), 1ff; see also Bafaqih, *L'Unification du Yemen antique,* 175ff. and 345ff; R. D. Tindel, in N. Nebes, ed., *Arabia Felix,* Festschrift for W. W. Müller (1994), 273ff.

141. This is more or less agreed on in the relevant literature. Pirenne, however, assumes on the basis of paleographic criteria that there were two different main eras—the Sabaean, starting around 110 B.C. and the Ḥimyar, starting around 115 B.C.; see *PSAS* 4 (1974), 118. For critical remarks on this, see Beeston, *PSAS* 11 (1981), 1ff.; also see von Wissmann, *ANRW* II, 9.1, 418ff. His remarks on p. 419, note 235d on Pirenne's dating are not all correct, however; see also Robin, *L'Arabie antique*, 15, 151, who supports the date of 110 B.C.

142. According to von Wissmann, *ANRW* II, 9.1, 421.

143. According to Müller, *Jemen Katalog,* 53.

144. See this chapter, note 136 above.

145. See *Arabien* (1963), 24.

146. See *Jemen Katalog,* 128.

147. See *Die Geschichte von Saba',* part I, 53-54, 85-86; Ephe'al, *Ancient Arabs,* 63-64, also regards this visit as "highly probable."

148. See E. A. Knauf, *Ismael. Untersuchungen zur Geschichte Palästinas und Nordarabiens im 1. Jahrtausand v. Chr.* (1985), 5. See also Hommel, in *Handbuch der altarabischen Altertumskunde,* ed. D. Nielsen, 65-66. J. A. Montgomery, *Arabia and the Bible* (1934), 180-81.

149. *Jemen Katalog,* 50; similarly, Beeston, *EI* 8 (1995), 665.

150. On this, see von Wissmann, *Die Geschichte von Saba',* part I, 53-54.

151. See A. Cavigneaux and B. K. Ismail in *Baghdader Mitteilungen* 21 (1990), 32ff. [339, 351, 357].

152. See *Yemen. Studi archeologici, storici e filologici sull'Arabia meridionale* 1 (1992), 111ff; see also H. D. Galter, *Studies in Oriental*

Culture and History, Festschrift W. Dostal, ed. A. Gangrich et al. (1993), 29ff.

153. According to Hommel in *Handbuch der altarabischen Altertumskunde,* ed. D. Nielsen (1927), 60, 151, 161-62, 180; Müller believes that the Sabaeans migrated from northeastern Arabia, i.e., from the region at the Arabian-Persian Gulf, see *Jemen Katalog,* 50.

154. *JEOL* 15 (1957-58), 242, note 12.

155. *ANRW* II, 9.1, 342, note 67; somewhat different in *Die Geschichte von Saba',* part II, 59-60.

156. See p. 36.

157. Translated from the German translation—the text of which follows—by W. W. Müller in O. Kaiser, ed., *Texte aus der Umwelt des Alten Testaments,* vol. 1, no. 6 (1985), 651ff.: "... und er es [d.h., Ausan] in Wusr [die Hauptstadt . . . steht für das ausanische Reich] schlug, bis er Ausan und seinen König Muratta'um hinwegfegte; und die Oberhäupter der Ratsversammlung von Ausan hatten es [Ausan] für Samahat [möglicherweise (die) Hauptgöttin von Ausan] bestimmt, er [Karib'il] aber bestimmte es zur Tötung und Gefangenschaft; und (als) er die Zerstörung seines [d.h., des ausanischen Königs] Palastes Maswar [Name des königlichen Palastes in Ausan] veranlaṣte und die Entfernung aller Inschriften, welche [Karib]'il bezeichnet hatte, aus seinem Palast [Maswar] und der Inschriften der Tempel seiner Götter und er . . . seinen Palast Maswar und die Kinder des Almaqah [eine Bezeichnung für die Sabäer] und die Stämmekonföderation, seine Freien und seine Sklaven, aus den Gebieten von Ausan und seiner Städte zurückführte. . . ."

See also N. Nebes, *Vienna Catalogue,* 165ff.

158. See *ANRW* II, 9.1, 340; see also *Die Geschichte von Saba',* part I, 89ff., 104-5; here, von Wissmann is more cautious. See also R. Fattovich, in *PSAS* 7 (1977), 73ff., where he rejects the notion of Saba' having directly colonized Abssynia. See also Bafaqih, *L'Unification du Yemen antique,* 253ff.

159. For example, W.F. Albright in a letter to von Wissmann (see note 158 above) and G. Van Beek, *Biblical Archaeologist* 5 (1952), 6.

160. See *Paléographie,* 151; see also A. Caquot and A.J. Drewes in *Annales des Ethiopie* 1 (1955), 26, 30; Drewes, *BiOr* 13 (1956), 179ff., [180, note 15].

161. According to Müller, *Jemen Katalog,* 50.

162. CIH = Corpus Inscriptionem Semiticarum, Pars Quarta (Himyariticas continens), in Paris, inscription publication starting in 1889.

163. On this, see Robin, *Jemen Katalog,* 77.

164. See note 32 in this chapter.

165. See *Jemen Katalog,* 77.

166. Von Wissmann, *Die Geschichte von Saba',* part II (1982), 46 dates the inscription at "approximately 510 B.C."

167. See p. 49 above.

168. Von Wissmann, op. cit., see also here, ch. 3, p. 19.

169. See pp. 48ff above.

170. This date is mentioned in von Wissmann, *Die Geschichte von Saba',* part II, 351; *ANRW* II, 9.1, 374; Pirenne, *Paléographie,* 177, dates it at around 300 B.C.

171. Von Wissmann, *ANRW* II, 9.1, 362.

172. Von Wissmann, ibid., 381.

173. See Müller, "Weihrauch," in *RE,* supp. vol. 15 (1978), 725.

174. According to Müller in *Jemen Katalog,* 52.

175. This report is supposed to have been written by the commander of the army Aelius Gallus, who led the Roman campaign against the South Arabian kingdoms, according to von Wissmann, *ANRW* II, 9.1, 467; on the other hand, Juba is generally viewed as Pliny's main source; see K. Sallmann in *Der kleine Pauly,* vol. 4 (1972), col. 932.

176. According to, for example, von Wissmann, *Le Muséon* 77 (1964), 429ff., *ANRW* II, 9.1, 420. Other authors too do not indicate two groups of Himyar; see Doe, *Southern Arabia* and Müller, *Jemen Katalog,* 50ff.

177. *PSAS* 5 (1975), 1ff.

178. Von Wissmann and M. Höfner, *Beiträge,* 315.

179. *ANRW* II, 9.1, 418; see also Beeston, *PASA* 11 (1981), 1ff.

180. See section 3 in this chapter.

181. See von Wissmann, *ANRW* II, 9.1, 436-37; Müller, *Jemen Katalog,* 52; and Beeston, *PSAS* 5 (1975), 4ff.

182. On this campaign, see von Wissmann, *ANRW* II, 9.1, 308ff.; many additional references are listed there; see more recently, C. Marek, *Chiron. Mitt. der Kommission E: Alte Geschichte und Epigraphik des Deutschen Arch. Inst.* 23 (1991), 121ff.

183. Strabo, *Geography* XVI, iv, 24.

184. See W. Aly, *Strabonis Geographica* 4 (1957), 165ff., von Wissmann, *ANRW* II, 9.1, 313; the years 26-25 B.C. are also mentioned; see, for example, S. Jameson, *Journal of Roman Studies* 58 (1968), 71ff.; and B. Bowersock, *Roman Arabia* (1983), 46.

185. See p. 50 above; on the history of South Arabia from the first century A.D. to the Islamic period, see W. W. Müller in *Studies,* 125ff.

186. According to von Wissmann, 441.

187. *Natural History* VI, xxv, 104.

188. See Müller, op. cit., 125; von Wissmann,"Zur Geschichte und Landeskunde von Alt-Südarabien," *Sammlung Eduard Glaser* 3: 43, 47, 75; J. Ryckmans, *La Chronologie de Rois de Saba et Du-Raydan,* Uitgaven van het Nederlands (Historical-archaeological institute of Istanbul)15 (1964).

189. See *L'Arabie antique*, 52ff.; similarly, see Bafaqih in *L'Unification du Yémen antique,* 1. However, he assumes there were three periods: "La haute période" (up to the first century B.C.), "Période intermédiaire" (commencing with the emergence of the Ḥimyarites and reaching its zenith in the unification of the kingdoms of Saba' and Ḥimyar), and "La basse période" (emergence of foreign powers such as Persia and Ethiopia).

190. See von Wissmann, *ANRW* II, 9.1, 438, and especially Robin, *L'Arabie antique,* 71ff. [78ff.].

191. See Müller, *Studies,* 126.

192. On this, see C. Robin, *Proceedings of the 8th Intern. Conf. of Ethiopian Studies* 2 (1989), 147ff.

193. Published by A. Jamme, *Sabaean Inscriptions from Maḥram Bilqîs (Mârib),* Publications of the American Foundation for the Study of Man 3 (1962); cited in relevant publications as "Jamme 550-850."

194. See Robin, *CRAI* (1981), 319ff.

195. According to Müller, *Jemen Katalog,* 53; Von Wissmann, *ANRW* II, 9.1, 444, dates it around 270.

196. Robin, *CRAI* (1981), 337; Müller in *Jemen Katalog,* 53; Bafaqih, *L'Unification du Yémen antique,* 136, refers to the year 281.

197. Müller, 127 dates it in the last or next to last decade of the third century; von Wissmann, 44, dates it around 300.

198. According to Müller, op. cit.

199. According to von Wissmann in: H. von Wissmann and M. Höfner, *Beiträge,* 334, note 5; there he refers to J. Ryckmans, who considers Yamanat to be western Yemen.

200. *Beiträge,* 335-36.

201. See *Neue Ephemeris für semitische Epigraphik* 2 (1974), 156ff.

202. According to Müller, *Jemen Katalog,* 53; see also Müller in *Al-Hudud,* Festschrift Maria Höfner (1981), 225ff. [248ff.].

203. According to Müller, ibid., and Robin, *L'Arabie antique,* 66. Von Wissmann, on the other hand, holds the view (in "Zur Geschichte und Landeskunde von Alt-Südarabien," *Sammlung Eduard Glaser* 3: 204, note 461) that this break in the dam preceded the three breaks already known); elsewhere ("Ḥimyar," *Le Muséon* 77 [1964], 491) he maintained that the inscription Ja 671 describes the second known break in the dam.

204. See Robin, *L'Arabie antique,* 144ff. In Chelhod, *L'Arabie du Sud. Histoire et civilisation* 1 (1984), 214, he still assumed that Malikkarib Yuhaʾmin had converted to Judaism. On the emergence of monotheism, see Beeston, *Studies*, 149ff.

205. On the dating of ʿĒzānā, see H. Brakmann, *Die Einwurzelung der Kirche im spätantiken Reich von Aksum* (1994), 67ff.

206. According to J. Ryckmans *L'Institution Monarchique,* 214, it was between 341 and 346. In Müller, *Reallexikon* 15 (1991), col. 307, it was around 340-342.

207. According to J. Ryckmans, *L'Institution Monarchique,* 215, this was Malikkarib Yuhaʾmin.

208. According to Müller, *Reallexikon,* col. 307.

209. According to Müller, *Jemen Katalog,* 53.

210. See Müller, *Jemen Report* 5-9 (1974), 2.

211. See Robin, *L'Arabie antique,* 144ff.; Beeston, *Studies,* 151; and M. Lecker, *Die Welt des Orients* 26 (1995), 139ff.

212. See *Beiträge,* 338, note 4.

213. See Robin, *L'Arabie antique,* 71ff.

214. According to Müller, *Jemen Katalog,* 53-54; see also von Wissmann, "BADW" in *EI* 1 (1959), 880ff.

215. Robin, *L'Arabie antique,* 81.

216. According to Müller, *Jemen Katalog,* 54; similarly, U. Brunner,

ABADY 2 (1983), 113; Robin, 66 gives the date as 456.

217. Müller, *Reallexikon* 15, col. 308-9.

218. See Müller, *Reallexikon,* col. 311, *Jemen Katalog,* 54. See also Beeston, *PSAS* 15 (1985), 5.

219. See inscription: Jamme 1028.

220. On these events, see Brakmann, *Die Einwurzelung der Kirche im spätantiken Reich von Aksum,* 85ff; and Müller, *Reallexikon,* col. 313ff.

221. On this, see Brakmann, ibid., 85ff., and Müller, col. 312-13.

222. On these dates, see Brakmann, 86, note 443; Müller, col. 314; F. de Blois, *AAE* 1 (1990), 110ff., Robin, *L'Arabie antique,* 150ff.

223. On this campaign, see B. Rubin, *Das Zeitalter Justinians I.* (1980), 312ff.

224. This is the date given by Brakmann, 93. Müller, *Reallexikon,* col. 318, maintains that the reign of Ṣimyafaʿ seems to have lasted less that a decade.

225. Here he makes reference to the inscription CIH 541; see *Jemen Katalog,* 55; Robin, *PSAS* 18 (1988), 96 dated this inscription "March 544 or 549."

226. According to Müller in *Jemen Katalog,* 55.

227. See *Beiträge,* 339.

228. Robin, *L'Arabie antique,* 81.

229. Müller, *Studies,* 131, sets the date as 570; in the *Reallexikon,* col. 322, it is given as the beginning of the sixth decade of the sixth century.

230. Müller, *Jemen Katalog,* 55; H. L. Gottschalk, *Bustan,* no. 4 (1962), 3, speaks of thirteen elephants.

231. At the Council of Chalcedon in the year 451, the "Faith of Chalcedon" was promulgated, which described Christ as having two natures, divine and human, "without confusion, without change, without division," perfectly united in a single person.

232. In *Reallexikon,* col. 319, Müller offers a comprehensive description of Christianity in South Arabia as well as an extensive bibliography.

233. R. Bowen, *Archaeological Discoveries in South Arabia* (1958), 76, gives the year 575, which he precisely characterized as "approximately within one generation." Brunner, *ABADY* 2 (1983), 118, maintains a dating of "roughly around 580," based on his geomorphological investigations. Müller, *Jemen Katalog,* 56, refers to the beginning of the

seventh century.

234. See Brunner, 119.

235. Müller, *Jemen Katalog,* 119.

236. G. R. Smith, *PSAS* 20 (1990), 134-35.

237. On this final phase of the history of ancient South Arabia, see H.L. Gottschalk in *Bustan,* no. 4 (1962), 2ff.

238. See Robin, *L'Arabie antique,* 69.

239. A Greek named Hippalos is supposed to have discovered the "regular winds" (monsoon winds) in the early first century A.D., according to H. Preidler, *Der kleine Pauly* 2 (1967), col. 1153. This is the same century in which the famous seaman's handbook, *Periplus Maris Erythraei,* was written, which demonstrates the importance of sea travel.

240. According to Robin in J. Chelhod, ed., *L'Arabie du Sud,* vol. 1, 220ff., and J. Dayton, *PSAS* 5 (1975), 52ff. [58]. R. L. Raikes and U. Brunner reject this; see *ABADY* 2 (1983), 119.

241. See Robin, *L'Arabie antique,* 71ff.; on the general reasons, see also Müller, *Jemen Katalog,* 55. See also, more recently, M. Piotrovsky and P. Gentelle, *Vienna Catalogue,* 395ff, 399ff.

VI. Social Structures

1. See *Documentation for Ancient Arabia,* part 1 (1994), 132, 242.

2. See *L'Arabie antique,* 51.

3. *ANRW* II/9.1, 355.

4. *Jemen Katalog,* 77; according to Kitchen, 103: 365-350 B.C.

5. See Kitchen, 80; Beeston, *PSAS* 7 (1977), 6; Pirenne, *Paléographie,* 191.

6. See *L'Arabie antique,* 52.

7. See Müller, *Jemen Katalog,* 51; see ch. 5 above, pp. 58ff.

8. See the references listed in ch. 5, note 21, especially *Reports and Memoirs* 24; see, recently, de Maigret, *Vienna Catalogue,* 117ff. and 157ff.

9. See W. Daum, ed., *Die Königin von Saba* (1988), 39.

10. See B. Vogt, *Jemen-Report* 27/1 (1996), 9; more recently, see Vogt and Sedov, *Vienna Catalogue,* 129ff.

11. See de Maigret, "The bronze age culture of Hawlan at-Tiyal and al-Hada," *Reports and Memoirs* 24 (1990), 200.

12. See ch. 5 above, p. 47.

13. See de Maigret, *Vienna Catalogue,* 157ff.; see also the article by W. Dostal, "Towards a Model of Cultural Evolution," in *Studies,* 185ff.; and Beeston, "Functional Significance of the Old South Arabian 'Town'," in *PSAS* 1 (1971), 26ff.

14. See ch. 5 above, p. 54, and esp. Robin, *Jemen Katalog,* 77, and J. Ryckmans, *L'Institution Monarchique,* 51ff.

15. See Ryckmans, 64ff.

16. See Beeston, *PSAS* 7 (1977), 5ff.

17. See Beeston, "The Warfare in Ancient South Arabia (2nd-3rd centuries A.D.)," in *Qahtan, Studies in the Old South Arabian Epigraphy,* fascicle 3 (1976), 26.

18. See the work by J. Ryckmans, *L'Institution Monarchique;* for Maʿīn, see Robin, "La Cité et l'Organisation Sociale à Maʿīn: L'Example de YIL (Aujourd'hui Barāqish)" *Studies,* 157ff.

19. *PSAS* 7 (1977), 7.

20. On the position of the kabīr, see J. Ryckmans, *PSAS* 2 (1971), 24; Beeston, *Epigraphic South Arabian Calendars and Dating* (1956), 25ff.; Grohmann, *Arabien,* 130; Robin in N. Nebes, ed., *Arabia Felix.* Festschrift W.W. Müller (1994), 230ff.

21. The precise interpretation of the word *qayl* is disputed. See the extensive discussion in Robin, *Les Haute-Terres du Nord-Yemen avant l'Islam,* tome 1 (1982), 79ff.; Beeston, *Qahtan, Studies in the Old South Arabian Epigraphy,* fasc. 3 (1976), 4; and A. Korotayev, *Orientalia* 63 (1994), 63ff.

22. See Grohmann, *Arabien,* 130ff.

23. See Robin, *Studies,* 157; Beeston, *Journal of the Economic and Social History of the Orient* 15 (1972), 256ff. [262ff.]; Grohmann, *Arabien,* 126ff. speaks of a *Ständeversammlung* or estates council, but he also admits that large segments of the population were not included.

24. See J. Ryckmans, *L'Institution Monarchique,* 22, 124; N. Rhodonakis, in *Handbuch der altarabischen Altertumskunde,* ed. D. Nielsen (1927), 126; Grohmann, *Arabien,* 125.

25. In Robin, *Les Hauts-Terres,* tome 1, 74, the name "rgl" appears,, whereas Grohmann, *Arabien,* 123, refers to the "warrior caste" as "qsd." Robin

translated this as *paysans libre,* or free peasants.

26. This is the translation according to Grohmann, *Arabien,* 124. Robin, on the other hand, speaks of "clients."

27. This is according to Robin, 89. Grohmann, 125 speaks of "subjects" and maintains that "ʿbd" is not a subordinate class similar to slaves.

28. See *Journal of the Economic and Social History of the Orient* 15 (1972), 256ff. [257ff.]; "Shaʿb," *EI* 9 (1995), 150-51; Robin, *Les Hautes-Terres,* tome 1, 17, and Bafaqih, *L'Unification du Yemen antique,* 106, refer to "tribu"; see also A. Korotayev, *BSOAS* 57 (1994), 469ff.

29. I assume that the Dorian League refers to the Peloponnesian League under the leadership of Sparta.

30. See Beeston, *Qahtan,* fasc. 3 (1976), 4; see also Robin, *Studies,* 157ff., ——, *Les Hautes-Terres,* tome 1, 71ff., and ——, in P. Bonnefant, ed., *La Peninsula arabique d'aujourd'hui* vol. 2 (1982), 17ff.

VII. Economy

1. See ch. 5 above, pp. 49ff.

2. See ch. 1 above, pp. 3ff.

3. See Beeston, *Qahtan,* fascicle 3 (1976), 2.

4. Frankincense also grew on the island of Socotra, in Somaliland, and along the Coromandel coast of India; see W. W. Müller, "Weihrauch," in *RE,* suppl. vol. 15 (1978), col. 700ff. (This article remains the most definitive on incense and the incense trade.) Myrrh is also found in Eritrea and northern Abyssinia. On the course of the incense route, see also Beeston, *BSOAS* 42 (1979), 7ff.

5. See *The Biblical Archaeologist Reader* 2 (1964), 119; see also, Müller, "Weihrauch," col. 734-35. Another calculation amounted to 13 denares (Roman silver coins) per kilogram of highest quality frankincense. In contrast, the annual cost of living in the Roman Middle East at the time of Pliny (1st century A.D.) was approximately 100-140 denares; see D. Martinetz, K. Lohs, and J. Janzen, *Weihrauch und Myrrhe* (1989), 53.

6. In addition to the work by Müller, in preparing this section I also referred to G. Stubbe, "Der Handel in nabatäischer Zeit unter besonderer Berücksichtigung der Weihrauchstrasse und der Seewege," unpublished M.A. thesis (Göttingen, 1992).

7. See Beeston, *Qahtan,* fasc. 1 (1959), as well as Grohmann, *Arabien,* 139.

A document listing Minaean market regulations has also survived; see Beeston, *BSOAS* 41 (1978), 142ff.

8. See Beeston, *Qahtan,* fasc. 1.

9. See S. E. Sidebotham, in *L'Arabie préislamique*(1986), 13ff.; Müller, "Weihrauch," col. 724ff., 734-35.

10. There is some disagreement as to when and by whom the monsoon route was discovered. Pliny (Nat. Hist. VI, 100ff.) and the anonymous author of the *Periplus Maris Erythraei* (a handbook for the commercial sea trade in the Middle East) have attributed it to a Greek seaman named Hippalos (*Periplus* 57). From March to October a constant wind blew from the southwest in the latitudes north of the equator, making it possible to travel to India in a short time. The northeasterly monsoon that came in the winter (from November to February) facilitated the return journey. The date of the discovery might have been sometime between the first century B.C. and the first century A.D. See L. Casson, in *L'Arabie préislamique,* 187.

11. See M. F. Charlesworth, *Trade Routes and Commerce of the Roman Empire* (1961), 60; see also J. F. Salles, in *L'Arabie et ses mers bordières,* vol. 1: "Itineraires et voisinages," *Travaus de la Maison de l'Orient* 16 (Lyon, 1988), 95ff.

12. According to Müller, *RE,* suppl. vol. 15, "Weihrauch," col. 726; see also I. P. Kirwan, in *L'Arabie préislamique,* 432; and ʿAbd al-Ġanī ʿAlī Saʿīd in *AAE* 6 (1995), 272.

13. Probably the harbor of the city of Sumhuram, present-day Khōr Rōrī, roughly 30 miles east of Salalah (Oman), according to Müller, "Weihrauch", col. 727; Pirenne, *Journal of Oman Studies* 1 (1975), 81ff.; von Wissmann, "Das Weihrauchland Saʾkalān, Samārum und Mos-cha," *ÖAkWS* 324 (1979), 42ff.; F.P. Albright, *The American Archaeological Expedition in Dhofar, Oman, 1952-1953,* Publ. of the American Foundation for the Study of Man, vol. 6 (1982), 7. N. Groom, *AAE* 6 (1995), 180ff. claims that Khōr Rōrī and Moscha are not one and the same. See also A. Avanzini, *Vienna Catalogue,* 280.

14. See L. Casson, in *L'Arabie préislamique,* 187 n. 3; it should be noted, however, that the datings in this handbook for merchants and ship's captains extend into the third century, according to, for instance, von Wissmann, *ANRW* II/9.1, 434 and Pirenne, *Qatabān,* 176ff. (n. 201) and *Journal Asiatique* 1961, 441ff.

15. According to L. Casson, 190; see also N. Groom, *AAE* 6 (1995), 183ff.

16. See von Wissmann, *ANRW* II/9.1, 434-35.

17. See *Periplus,* § 24 and Casson, ibid. The following are very good editions of *Periplus:* H. Frisk, "Le Périple de la Mer Erythrée," *Göteborgs Högskalas Arsskrift* 33 (1927) and G. W. B. Huntingford, *The Periplus of the Erythraean Sea* (1980), and L. Casson, *The Periplus Maris Erythraei* (1989).

18. According to A. Dihle, *ANRW* II/9.2, 547.

19. See *Periplus,* 6, 24ff.

20. The exact location of Rhapta is uncertain. It might have been in the vicinity of the present-day Daressalam; see L. Casson, 191, and L. P. Kirwan, *L'Arabie préislamique,* 433.

21. See Casson, 192; on the Soviet excavations since 1985 in Qana, see A. V. Sedov in *AAE* 3 (1992), 110ff.; also in *Tradition and Archaeology. Early Maritime Contacts in the Indian Ocean,* ed. H. P. Ray and J. F. Salles (1996), 11ff.; and most recently, *Vienna Catalogue,* 275ff.

22. See *Periplus,* § 27ff.

23. See Charlesworth, *Trade-Routes and Commerce of the Roman Empire* (1961), 108-109.

24. See W. F. Albright, ed., *Archaeological Discoveries in South Arabia,* vol. 2, Publ. of the American Foundation for the Study of Man (1958).

25. See *Fouilles de Schabwa,* ed. J.-F. Breton, Institut Français d'Archéologie du Proche-Orient, *Publication Hors Série* 19 (1992). This report is virtually the same as the one by Breton et al. in *Syria* 68 (1991), 1-431.

26. See *Jemen Report* 5 (1974), 4ff., esp. "Agrargeographie der Arabischen Republik Jemen," *Erlanger Geographische Arbeiten,* special vol. 11 (1981); see also H. H. Siewert, *ABADY* 1 (1982), 181ff., M. Höfner, *Grazer Morgenländische Studien* 12 (1989), 343ff.

27. See Höfner, 347.

28. Incidentally, another crop cultivated today, the coffee tree, and thus the coffee bean, was not documented until the fifteenth-sixteenth centuries. Exactly when it was first systematically planted and cultivated and what must have preceded the coffee trade chronologically are not known (see H. Becker, V. Höhfeld, H. Kopp, "Kaffee aus Arabien," *Geographische Zeitschrift,* supplement no. 46 (1979), 7-8.

29. On this information, see Ingrid Hehmeyer, *ABADY* 5 (1991), 51ff. [54ff.].

30. See Hehmeyer, 54ff.; see also, A. Grohmann, *Südarabien als Wirtschaftsgebiet,* part one: "Osten und Orient," *Erste Reihe Forschungen* 4 (1922), 204 (Part two [1933] also provides valuable information).

VIII. Military

1. One of the most extensive reports is that of the Sabaean ruler Karibʾīl Watar (RES 3945), see pp. 57-58. Other inscriptions about battles and military campaigns can be found in Beeston, "Warfare in ancient South Arabia (2nd-3rd centuries A.D.)," *Qahtan,* Studies in old South Arabian Epigraphy, fasc. 3 (1976).
2. The military is treated neither in the *Jemen Katalog* nor in the numerous works by von Wissmann or the more recent book by C. Robin, *L'Arabie antique,* to mention only a few. In *AfO* 42-43 (1995-96), 503, Müller refers to a work in Arabic: al-Ḥāriṯī, S.b.A., *Ǧaiš al-Yaman qablal-Islām* (On the Military in Pre-Islamic Jemen), Sanaa 1991 [I did not have access to this work].
3. See note 1 in this chapter.
4. "Les Fortifications d'Arabie Méridionale du 7e au 1er siècle avant notre ère," *ABADY* 7.
5. On warfare in Mesopotamia, see F. Malbran-Labat, *L'armée et l'organ-isátion militaire de l'Assyrie d'après les lettres des Sargonides trouvées à Ninive,* Ecole Pratique des Hautes Etudes, sect. 4, Sciences historiques et philologiques, vol. 2, *Hautes etudes Orientales* 19 (Paris, 1982).
6. See Beeston, *Qahtan,* fasc. 3, 7ff.
7. According to Beeston, 19 n.14, the etymology of this word is somewhat puzzling.
8. Beeston appears to have changed his mind; in *Le Muséon* 65 (1952), 140-41 he maintained that a professional army could not have existed in South Arabia under the conditions at that time—in contrast to M. Hartmann, *Die arabische Frage* (1909), 448-49. Later, however, Beeston said (see *Qahtan,* fasc. 3 [1976], 7-8, 10) that in a certain sense the "Khamis" were a professional army; see also *BSOAS* 42 (1979), 10 n.13.
9. See ch. 6, p. 83 and note 21.
10. On this inscription, see W. W. Müller in *Al-Hudud,* Festschrift for Maria Höfner on her 80th birthday (1981), 225ff. [229, 237].
11. See Beeston, *Qahtan,* 9-10; see also Robin, *L'Arabie antique,* 78ff.
12. These figures were taken from Beeston, 24ff.
13. Ibid., 13.
14. According to M. Korfmann, *Schleuder und Bogen in Südwestasien. Von den frühesten Belegen bis zum Beginn der historischen Stadtstaaten,*

Antiquitas, 3rd ser., vol. 13 (1972), 217.

15. See M. Kazanski in J.-F. Breton and M. ʿAbd al-Qadir Bafaqih, eds., *Trésors du Wadi Dura,* Institut Français d'Archéologie du Proche-Orient, *Bibliothèque Arch. et Historique* 141 (1993), 51ff.

16. *Geogr.* 16/4, 24; see also Korfmann, 6, 8.

17. See K. G. Lindblom, *Die Schleuder in Afrika und anderwärts,* Riksmuseets Etnografiska Avdetning, *Smärre Meddelanden* 2 (1927), 28.

18. Beeston, *Qahtan,* 15-16.

19. *ABADY* 8 (1994), 166.

20. See Breton, 79ff., 171ff.

21. Breton referred to "casemate walls" (see p. 148), and to "murs faits d'edifices" ("compartment walls"). The compartments of the latter, formed by cross-walls, were filled with rough stones or earth. The casemate walls retained hollow spaces which the defenders could stand in or which could be used as living or storage space.

22. An extensive description of the city walls of Marib can be found in B. Finter, *ABADY* 3 (1986), 73ff.; see also Breton, 89ff.

23. See Breton, 159ff., 168, 185.

24. Breton, 172. The Germany summary has a question mark after the dating "first century B.C."; see 186.

25. The book by R. Naumann, *Architektur Kleinasiens von ihren Anfängen bis zum Ende der hethitischen Zeit* (2nd, expanded, edition 1971) clearly shows how advanced this region was even prior to "archaic" era in South Arabia.

IX. Religion

1. Following are relatively recent introductions to religion in ancient South Arabia: J. Ryckmans, "Die Altsüdarabische Religion," in *Jemen Katalog,* 111ff. and J. Ryckmans, "Religions of South Arabia," in D. N. Freedman, ed., *The Anchor Bible Dictionary,* vol. 6 (1992), 171ff. Other standard works are: Beeston, "The Religions of the Pre-Islamic Yemen," in J. Chelhod, ed., *L'Arabie du Sud,* vol. 1, 259ff; M. Höfner, "Die Religionen Altsyriens, Altarabiens und der Mandäer," in *Religionen der Menschheit* 10, 2 (1970), 234ff.; A. Jamme, "La religion arabe préislamique," in M. Brillant and R. Aigrain, eds., *Histoire des Religions* 4 (1956); G. Ryckmans, "Les religions arabes préislamique," *Bibliothèque*

du Muséon 26 (2nd ed., 1951); more recently, see also W. W. Müller, *Vienna Catalogue,* 205ff.

2. According to Beeston, *PSAS* 7 (1977), 5ff. [9].

3. *Al-Yaman* calendar (1991), reverse side of "October."

4. Jamme, "La religion arabe préislamique," 249ff. offers a good overview of the state of discourse on ancient South Arabian religion (only up to 1956).

5. According to J. Ryckmans, *Jemen Katalog,* 111.

6. See M. Höfner, "Die Religionen Altsyriens, Altarabiens und der Mandäer," 269, 352.

7. He is generally viewed as masculine. See, for example, G. Ryckmans, "Les religions arabes préislamique," 42; Grohmann, *Arabien,* 244; A. Jamme, "La religion arabe préislamique," 260ff. However, J. Ryckmans, *Jemen Katalog,* 111, indicated that it has recently been put forward that some of his symbols are sun symbols or references to Dionysos. Ryckmans adopted this opinion, viewing ʾAlmaqah as a sun god, a male form of the Goddess Shams.

8. J. Ryckmans, *Jemen Katalog,* 112, expressed uncertainty whether Wadd was identical to the moon god.

9. For Ryckmans, op. cit., he was to be viewed as a sun god.

10. *Al-Yaman* calendar (1991), reverse side of "October."

11. D. Nielsen repeatedly put forth the theory that the entire South Arabian pantheon could be traced back to this trinity; see *Handbuch der alt-arabischen Altertumskunde,* 227. Jamme's critique of this opinion is worthwhile reading; see "La religion arabe préislamique," 257ff.; see also M. Höfner, "Die Religionen Altsyriens, Altarabiens und der Mandäer," 245-46.

12. For example, see the well-known Sabaean inscription RES 4176. It includes a statute of the god Taʿlab of Riyam (town in Arhab in the northern Yemenite highlands) for his tribe Sumʾay. See W. W. Müller, in O. Kaiser, ed., *Texte aus der Umwelt des Alten Testaments,* vol. 2, part 3 (1988), 438ff. A new translation by Müller, including a commentary, appeared in *Aktualisierte Beiträge zum 1. Internationalen Symposium Südarabien* (The updated proceedings of the 1st Intern. Symposium on South Arabia), ed. R. G. Stiegner (Graz, 1997), 89-110.

13. In *Al-Hudud,* Festschrift Maria Höfner (1981), 263ff.

14. These presumably did exist, according to Grohmann, *Arabien,* 247. J.

Ryckmans, *Jemen Katalog,* 113, maintained that statues in human form did exist, but were very rare and came later. The following have denied the existence of idols in human form: J. Henninger, *Anthropos* 38-40 (1942-45), 804 and note 101; and M. Höfner, "Die Religionen Altsyriens, Altarabiens und der Mandäer," 333-34. According to Jamme, "La religion arabe préislamique," 295, the question cannot be answered on the basis of existing information; this has also be maintained by J. Schmidt, *Jemen Katalog,* 98.

15. See below, ch. 10, sec. 1b "Sacral architecture," for a detailed discussion of the architecture.

16. See J. Ryckmans, *Jemen Katalog,* 113, and Jamme, "La religion arabe préislamique," 292ff.

17. See note 12 in this chapter.

18. According to J. Ryckmans, *Jemen Katalog,* 114, prisoners in the Ḥimyar kingdom during the second and third centuries A.D. were ritually sacrificed to the goddess Shams. M. Höfner, "Die Religionen Altsyriens, Altarabiens und der Mandäer," 333ff., and H. Grimme, *Zeitschrift für Assyriologie* 29 (1914), 187, spoke of child sacrifices. Jamme, 296, on the other hand, expressed the view that the relevant text was read incorrectly; the same is true for G. Ryckmans, "Les religions arabes préislamique," 33. The following have maintained that no human sacrifices were made: M. Höfner, op. cit., and J. Henniger, in *Al-Hudud,* Festschrift Maria Höfner (1981), 65ff.

19. Extensive literature exists on this subject. See Müller, in O. Kaiser, ed., *Texte,* vol. 2, part 3, 442ff., and Müller, *ABADY* 3 (1986), 101ff.

20. On the excavations and their respective publications mentioned below, see ch. 4, "Exploration History."

21. See *ABADY* 1 (1982), 171ff.

22. This refers to above-ground, circular tombs, in which a cross-section shows a beehive-like shape.

23. Round structures with a cylindrical, pillbox shape.

24. A comprehensive report by J.-C. Roux on the excavation of such a cave in Shabwa can be found in *Syria* 68 (1991), 331ff.

25. In addition to the extensive article by Schmidt (see note 21), the two books by B. Doe, *Monuments of South Arabia* and *Southern Arabia,* offer further information.

26. Beeston, *Al-Yaman* calendar (1991), reverse side of "October."

27. See ch. 5, p. 63 and note 204, above.

28. This is indicated by Beeston, *Studies,* 151, and similarly, Müller, *Reallexikon,* col. 309. See also Robin, *L'Arabie antique,* 147; on the expression *"ḥanīf,"* see *EI* 3 (1979), 165-66.

29. See Beeston, op. cit., and Robin, 146-47; J. Ryckmans, "Le christianisme en Arabie du Sud préislamique," in *Accademia Nazionale dei Lincei anno 361. Atti del Convegno intern sul tema L'Oriente Christ* (Rome, 1964), 439, maintained that the "Rahmanism" of the fifth century was neither Jewish nor influenced by Judaism. Later, however, in *Jemen Katalog,* 115, he said, "from the end of the fourth century on, even personalities of high status professed the Jewish faith." However, I do not think this reveals anything about the religious leanings of Rahmanism.

30. On this, see Beeston and Robin, op. cit., as well as Müller, *Reallexikon,* col. 314ff.

31. See Robin, 148-49.

32. See Grohmann, *Arabien,* 252; on Islam in Yemen, see W. Madelung, *Jemen Katalog,* 172ff.

X. Art

1. See de Maigret, "Die Königin von Saba," in W. Daum, ed., 36, and Schmidt, *Jemen Katalog,* 81.

2. Once again, see the two essays by Beeston (ch. 5, sec. 3, note 108), wherein he rejects the expression "capital" or "urban center" in reference to the ancient South Arabian cities.

3. Müller, "Marib," *EI* 6 (1990), 559; Grohmann, *Arabien,* 142, referred to 282 acres (114 ha) and according to von Wissmann, *Le Muséon* 75 (1962), 193, it was only 173 acres (70 ha).

4. R. Le Baron Bowen, Jr., in *Archaeological Discoveries in South Arabia,* 5: 52 acres; von Wissmann, *Le Muséon* 75 (1962), 193: 59 acres (24 ha) with additional figures regarding the sizes of other locations. Doe, *Monuments of South Arabia,* 126, referred to 41 acres (16.6 ha), but on p. 129, there is reference to 52-59 acres (incorrectly converted here to 37 ha).

5. Breton, *Syria* 68 (1991): 37 acres (15 ha); von Wissmann, op. cit.: 39.5 acres (16 ha).

6. The figure were taken from Joan Oates, *Babylon* (1979), 144.

7. See R. McC. Adams, *Land behind Baghdad* (1963), 144.

8. See R. Naumann, *Architektur Kleinasiens,* 2nd, expanded ed. (1971), 213.

9. According to Grohmann, *Arabien,* 140; see also Doe, *Monuments of South Arabia,* 117ff., which includes numerous city plans.

10. For further examples, see Grohmann, op. cit.

11. This figure for the length was taken from Breton, *ABADY* 8 (1994), 19. Here, Breton also included lengths for other cities. The German summary referred to almost 2.8 mi (4500 m) in length. B. Finster, *ABADY* 3 (1986), 73ff. did not mention any figures at all in her article "Die Stadtmauer von Marib."

12. In this context please refer to the ch. 8 "The Military" and the work by Breton cited numerous times.

13. See C. Darles, *Syria* 68 (1991), 77ff.

14. The Yemenite scholar al-Hamdānī (died 945-46 A.D.) offered several descriptions of castles in the eighth volume of his work *Iklīl.* See D. H. Müller, "Die Burgen und Schlösser Südarabiens nach dem *Iklīl* des Hamdānī," vol. 1, *ÖAkWS* 94 (1879), 335ff.; vol. 2, *ÖAkWS* 97 (1880), 955ff., and L. Forrer, "Südarabien nach al-Hamdani's Beschreibung der Arabischen Halbinsel," *Dt. Morgenl. Ges., Abb. zur Kunde des Morgenl* 27/3 (1942).

15. See Breton, *Syria* 68 (1991), 209ff.; W. W. Müller, "Shabwa," *EI* 9 (1995), 165ff.

16. It is considered a temple by the excavators (see Van Beek, *The Biblical Archaeologist* 15 [1952], 10ff., and W. Philipps, *Qataban and Sheba* [1955], 170ff.) and, at first, by Doe as well, in Doe, *Southern Arabia*, 26, 218ff. (he later referred to it as a "palace," see *PSAS* 14 [1984], 21), whereas Jamme, *BASOR* 138 (1955), 39, considered it a public building used by the king.

17. pp. 222ff.; also M. Jung, *AION* 48 (1988), 186, note 14.

18. See pp. 47.

19. The German Archaeological Institute in Sanaa publishes the *Archäologische Berichte aus dem Yemen,* ABADY, which provides the best information. Müller's article in *EI* 6 (1990), 559ff. is a good supplement. For a good overview, see also J. Schmidt, "Die sabäische Wasserwirtschaft von Marib," in *Jemen Katalog,* 57ff.

20. According to Schmidt, *Jemen Katalog,*60, and von Wissmann, *ANRW* II, 9.1, 355.

21. There is considerable variance in the measurements: Grohmann, *Arabien*, 151: 577.5 m. (almost 1900 ft.); Doe, *Southern Arabia,* 76: 1800 ft.; Robin, *L'Arabie antique,* 65: 650 m. (over 2100 ft.); W.W. Müller, *EI* 6 (1991), 563: 620 m. (2035 ft.) long, 16 m. (52.5 ft.) high, and 60 m. (197 ft.) wide.

22. See *Jemen Katalog,* 62.

23. See ch. 5, sec. 4, p. 67.

24. See the report by P. Gentelle in *Syria* 68 (1991), 5ff.

25. See Grohmann, *Arabien,* 148ff.; see also the various reports on irrigation systems in the *ABADY* volumes; on dams, see Doe, *Monuments of South Arabia,* 184ff. No reference points exist to facilitate dating of the tanks in Aden.

26. See Grohmann, 146ff.

27. See G. Ryckmans, *Le Muséon* 62 (1949), 74-75, and *PSAS* 6 (1976), 69ff; see also Grohmann, *Arabien,* 146 and von Wissmann, *Beiträge,* 263-64, though the measurements there are incorrect. Von Wissmann simply changed Groom's foot-measurements into meters! Two photographs of the pass route can be seen in Lankester Harding, *Archaeology in the Aden Protectorates,* plate 47, pp. 4-5. Inscriptions along the pass have revealed even the name of the architect–chief engineer, Awsam bin Yasurram, and the ancient name of the pass, Mablaqat.

28. See *PSAS* 6 (1976), 69ff.

29. For photographs of this pass route, see Lankester Harding, plate 49, pp. 1-5.

30. See Grohmann, *Arabien,* 146-47, especially with reference to the surveys conducted by von Wissmann. See also M. Gering, in *ABADY* I (1982), 43.

31. A. von Wrede, who in 1843 was the first European to see the wall, called the site Obne. Later visitors knew it under the name Libna. According to Doe, *Southern Arabia,* 181, the correct name is al-Mabna. Other names that exist for it are el-Bana and Qalat.

32. For a translation, see Doe, *Southern Arabia,* 181.

33. According to von Wissmann, *Beiträge,* 314, it was before the end of the fifth century B.C. In *ANRW* II, 9.1, 448, it is dated 10 B.C. And in Grohmann, *Arabien,* 155, it is the third century B.C.

34. According to Doe, *Southern Arabia,* 182, and Grohmann, ibid.; von Wissmann, *Beiträge,* 312, set the height at up to approximately 23 feet. In contrast to Doe, von Wissmann did not personally visit the site.

35. Whereas von Wissmann and Grohmann wrote that the blocks were supposedly held together with a cementlike mortar, Doe (182) reported that they were laid dry (without mortar) and well bonded. Two excellent photographs of the wall have been reproduced in Doe, plates 79-80.

36. See *Beiträge,* 313; and Doe, *Monuments of South Arabia,* 182, 184.

37. See *ABADY* 1, 161; in this context it should be noted that Pirenne's criticism (*Syria* 61 [1984]) of this volume in general, and the essay on temple architecture by Schmidt in particular, went too far ("Apparemment peu familiarisé avec la véritable pratique funéraires des Sud-Arabes anciens, J. Schmidt nous présente..."). As the irony of fate had it, Pirenne's critique of von Wissmann's "Long Chronology" (see *Syria,* 130ff.) soon proved false and over the years, based on more recent archaeological finds, some of her "supporters" have switched to the "Long Chronology" camp.

38. *Arabien,* 157ff.

39. M. Jung, "The Religious Monuments of Ancient Southern Arabia. A Preliminary Typological Classification," in *AION* 48 (1988), 177ff. The article is a summary of the author's doctoral dissertation of 1986; see also, recently, C. Darles, *Vienna Catalogue,* 209ff.

40. See Jung, 203ff.

41. *Jemen Katalog,* 81.

42. See *Jemen Katalog,* 81; similarly, Jung, 182.

43. See Schmidt, *Jemen Katalog,* 82; *ABADY* 4 (1987), 143ff.

44. Jung, 179ff.

45. For examples, see Schmidt in both works. In Jung, 179ff., category A "Rock Sanctuaries" is followed by level B "Sanctuaries with rectangular ground plan," whereby this category is also subdivided.

46. According to Schmidt, *Jemen Katalog,* 83. An additional reference for this section was the master's thesis by Regina Heck of the University of Göttingen: "The Temple and its Significance in the Ancient Southwest Arabian Cultural Sphere" (1981).

47. See *ABADY* 1 (1982), 91ff. and 4 (1987), 179ff.

48. See *ABADY* 1 (1982), 135ff.

49. See *ABADY* 1 (1982), 165. Schmidt assumed that the so-called entrance hall of the sanctuary was based on an older structure, a rectangular temple of hypaethral design, to which the oval wall was later attached; similarly, Jung, 202, assigned this building to category C2 "Enclosures with

monumental annexe."

50. There is also one example of this type on Minaean territory, namely, the RAṢF ʿAṯtar temple near Maʿīn.

51. See *Jemen Report* 27/1 (1996), 8; also Vogt, *Vienna Catalogue,* 219ff.

52. See *Jemen Katalog* 85; *ABADY* 1, 165ff.

53. See also the following description of the temples in the Ḥaḍramaut. Accordingly, I would consider this building to be one of the "terrace temples."

54. Details on this temple can be found in the report by C. Robin, J.-F. Breton and R. Audouin, *Syria* 56 (1976), 425ff.; Robin, *CRAI* (1979), 193ff.; and Jung, 196.

55. See de Maigret, *PSAS* 21 (1991), 159ff., and de Maigret, *Vienna Catalogue,* 217. The French discovered another temple dedicated to Nakraḥ near Baraqīsh at Darb aṣ-Ṣabī; see Robin, Breton and J. Ryckmans in *Raydan* 4 (1981), 249ff.

56. On these surveys, see Breton, *Syria* 56 (1979), 427ff.; *PSAS* 10 (1980), 5ff.; *CRAI* (1980), 57ff. *Raydan* 2 (1979), 185ff. includes a report on the excavation of one of these temples, namely, the temple of Bā-Quṭfah; see also A.V. Sedov, *PSAS* 24 (1994), 183ff.

57. In *ABADY* 1 (1982), 169, Schmidt still spoke of style phases. In the *Jemen Katalog* (1987), 97, on the other hand, he thought a division into style phases was premature.

58. Jung, 207ff.

59. See Jung, 210.

60. See note 14 above.

61. Statues are any figures larger than half a life-size human form, i.e., larger than roughly 30-33 inches. Smaller figures are referred to as statuettes. See U. Jantzen, *dtv-Lexikon der Antike,* vol. 2: Kunst (1970), 293.

62. See *L'Arabie préislamique,* 281, 285. This essay, "Bemerkungen zu den archäologischen Beziehungen zwischen Südarabien und dem griechisch-römischen Kulturkreis," as well as Almut Hauptmann–von Gladiss, "Probleme altsüdarabischer Plastik" in *Baghdader Mitt.* 10 (1979), 145ff., and E. Will, "De la Syrie au Yemen: Problèmes de relations dans le domaine de l'art" in *L'Arabie préislamique,* 271, provide a good introduction to the subject. Finally, see Grohmann, *Arabien* 218ff. (though it is somewhat outdated); Pirenne, *La Grèce et Saba,* 139ff.; Doe, *Southern Arabia,* 106-115; and de Maigret, *Arabia Felix,* Festschrift for W. W. Müller, 142ff.

63. See also Pirenne, 151-52.

64. See Will, *Vienna Catalogue,* 281ff.

65. For a good presentation of this restoration work and the problems associated with it, see K. Weidemann, *Könige aus dem Yemen* (1983). See also K. Parlasca, 283-85 and E. Will, *L'Arabie préislamique,* 271ff.

66. Weidemann's interpretation (18) is not entirely correct; see Müller, *PSAS* 9 (1979), 79.

67. See Weidemann, Parlasca, Will, and Müller, op. cit.

68. According to Weidemann, 18. A find in Shabwa might represent a parallel case. There, a fragment of a bronze horse was found. Parts of the South Arabian inscription refer to a local caster, but the craftsman could have come from the Mediterranean area. See R. Andouin, *Syria* 68 (1991), 175, 181.

69. According to Weidemann, op. cit; and Parlasca, 284.

70. According to Hauptmann–von Gladiss, 166.

71. See Andouin, *Syria* 68 (1991), 174ff.

72. See illustrations in *Archaeological Discoveries in South Arabia,* 283ff.

73. See Hauptmann–von Gladiss, 146-47, which includes numerous additional references.

74. See Will, 272-73 and Parlasca, 282-83, both in *L'Arabie préislamique;* B. Segall in *Archaeological Discoveries,* 155ff.; Pirenne, *Qatabān,* 45ff.

75. On this find, see Parlasca, 284; Grohmann, *Arabien,* 231. There is an excellent photograph in the *Jemen Katalog,*45ff.

76. See F.P. Albright, *The American Arch. Expedition in Dhofar, Oman 1952-1953,* Publ. of the American Foundation for the Study of Man, vol. 6 (1982), 101, no. 137, illus. plate 32, fig. 58; Höfner, *AfO* 17 (1954-56), 470.

77. See plate 28, 1-4 in Hauptmann–von Gladiss.

78. 156-57, 164ff.

79. See F. P. Albright in *Archaeological Discoveries in South Arabia,* 273, nos. 49-63.

80. On the various works of art, see Grohmann, *Arabien,* 238ff.; on glyptic, see D. Pickworth, *Vienna Catalogue,* 202ff.

81. Several examples have been uncovered by the French excavations in Shabwa; see R. Audouin, *Syria* 68 (1991), 167ff.; as well as by the excavation by von Wissman and C. Rathjens in the temple of Huqqa; see

Rathjens and von Wissmann, *Vorislamische Altertümer;* Rathjens and von Wissmann, *Südarabienreise,* vol. 2 (1932), 57ff., figs. 25, 26.

82. See J.-F. Breton and M. ʿAbd al-Qādir Bāfaqīh, eds., *Trésors du Wadi Dura.* République du Yemen. Fouille franco-yéménite de la nécropole de Hajar am-Dhaybiyya. Institut Français d'Archéologie du Proche-Orient. *Bibliothèque Archéologique et Historique* 141 (1993). For an extensive discussion of this book, see W. W. Müller, *AfO* 42-43 (1995-96), 296ff.

83. See the essays by Breton in *L'Arabie préislamique*, 173ff.; and Andouin, *Syria* 68 (1991), 165ff. and E. Will, 183ff.

84. See *Sabaeica* (1955), part 2, 86ff.

85. See *Baghdader Mitt.* 10 (1979), 147; see also the article by P. Costa in *Yemen. Studi archeologici, storici e filologici sull'Arabia meridionale* 1 (1992), 19ff., which mentions important information on some iconographic motifs of ancient South Arabian art.

86. See G. Dembski, "Die Münzen der Arabia Felix" in *Jemen Katalog,* 132ff.; ——, in A. Janata, ed., *Yemen: Im Land der Königin von Saba* (1989), 106. See also G. F. Hill, *Proceedings of the British Academy 1915-1916,* 79ff.; ——-, *Catalogue of the Greek Coins of Arabia, Mesopotamia and Persia,* British Museum (1922), lvii; Pirenne, *La Grèce et Saba,* 162ff.; A.K. Irvine, *Journal of the Royal Asiatic Society* (1964), 18ff.; Doe, *Southern Arabia,* 118ff.; S.C.H. Munro-Hay, *Syria* 68 (1991), 393ff.; A.V. Sedov, *AAE* 3 (1992), 110ff.; ——, *AAE* 6 (1995), 15ff.; A. V. Sedov and B. Davidde, *Vienna Catalogue,* 195ff.

87. See R. Göbl, *Antike Numismatik* 1 (1978), 146ff.

88. Dembski, 132.

89. According to Pirenne, *La Grèce et Saba,* 162; see also A. V. Sedov and B. Davidde, *Vienna Catalogue,* 196: early fourth century.

90. According to Dembski, 132, it began in the early third century B.C.; according to Doe, 119, it was the mid-third century B.C.

91. According to A. V. Sedov and U. Aydarus, *AAE* 6 (1995), 40.

92. According to Dembski, 134; Munro-Hay, 407, mentions a "head pronouncedly semitic."

93. According to Dembski, 134. According to Munro-Hay, 407, not until the first century A.D.

94. According to Dembski, 134, the "bucranium series" replaced the Augustan head series. Munro-Hay, 407, on the other hand, said that the two series overlapped in part, existing simultaneously.

95. According to Munro-Hay, 407.

96. At least according to Doe, *Southern Arabia,* 121. Munro-Hay, 410: coin minting ended after the end of the Qatabān kingdom. But when was that? According to Pirenne it was around 250 A.D., according to W. F. Albright it was 50 B.C. Dembski (135) wrote: "South Arabian coins stopped being minted when the Axumites assumed power." But that would not have been until around 525 A.D.; Pirenne, *Qatabān,* 64, names the year 300 A.D. as the date of the last Ḥimyar coins with heads on both sides. More recently, in Munro-Hay, *Vienna Catalogue,* 200: "Coin production in Saba', Ḥimyar, and Ḥaḍramaut appears to have already come to an end a half century before all of South Arabia was conquered by Ḥimyar around 275."

97. Hill, *Proceedings,* 58, had already said that; see also M. Mitchiner, *Oriental Coins and their Values: The Ancient and Classical World 600 B.C.-A.D. 650,* 95.

98. See, for example, Hill, *Catalogue of the Greek Coins of Arabia, Mesopotamia and Persia,* British Museum (1922), 75; Doe, *Southern Arabia,* 119-122 and plate 44. For Maʿīn, see Hill, *Proceedings,* 80ff. According to A.V. Sedov and U. Aydarus, *AAE* 6 (1995), 37, to date there have been no gold or silver coins found in Ḥaḍramaut that can unequivocally be regarded as Ḥaḍramaut mintings.

99. Doe, *Southern Arabia,* 119; on the other hand, Barbara Davidde, *AAE* 6 (1995), 255, expressed the view that the names Ḥarīb or Raydān do not refer to the mints; instead, only the political and economic power of the minting authority was supposed to be emphasized.

100. Doe, *Southern Arabia,* 119.

101. Irvine, 23 note 2, 33-34.

102. *Catalogue,* LVII, 54.

103. Dembski, 134.

104. See Munro-Hay, *Syria* 68 (1991), 393ff. as well as the comprehensive article by Sedov and Aydarus, *AAE* 6 (1995), 15ff.

105. See Sedov and Aydarus, ibid., and Sedov *AAE* 3 (1992), 110ff. and 177ff.

106. See P. Griaznevich, *Nataidj amal al-bathaa li-am* (1989) (Sayun, Yemen, 1990), and Sedov, *AAE* 6, 41-2 and 50.

107. See F.P. Albright, *The American Archaeological Expedition in Dhofar, Oman,* 90-92, plates 40-41, figs. 81-83.

108. See Munro and Hay, 393; Dembski, 135; M. Mitchiner, *Oriental Coins and their Values: The Ancient and the Classical World 600 B.C.-A.D. 650* (1978), 95; Doe, *Southern Arabian,* 119. Sedov and Aydarus, *AAE* 6 (1995), 37ff., said this is merely due to chance with respect to the find situation.

109. Doe, *Southern Arabia,* 120.

110. Irvine, 35.

111. *AAE* 6, 40 and 50.

112. Dembski, 135.

113. See also Grohmann, *Arabien,* 238.

114. G. C. Thompson, *The Tombs and Moon Temple of Hureidha (Hadramaut)* (1944).

115. See above, ch. 5, note 84.

116. See L. Badre, *Syria* 68 (1991), 229ff., as well as the critical remarks by G. Van Beek, *BASOR* 293 (1994), 91.

117. See here ch. 5, note 14.

118. Sedov, *AAE* 3 (1992), 110ff.; and H. P. Ray and J. F. Salles, eds., *Tradition and Archaeology* (1996), 11ff.

119. According to Van Beek, *Hajar bin Humeid,* 79ff.

120. This explanation has been adopted by M. R. Toplyn, a member of the American Wadi al-Jūbah project; see *The Wadi al-Jubah Archaeological Project,* vol. 1 (1984), 50, 68.

121. See Van Beek, 86-87; Toplyn, ibid.; and Doe, *Southern Arabia,* 117.

122. *Syria* 68 (1991), 277.

123. *Sabaeica* 2 (1955), 176.

124. *The American Arch. Expedition in Dhofar,* 92.

125. Sedov, *AAE* 6 (1995), 103ff. [108, 110].

126. See W. D. Glanzman and A. O. Ghaleb, *The Wadi al-Jūbah Archaeological Project,* vol. 3 (1987), 68.

127. See Sedov, *AAE* 3 (1992), 112; and *Tradition and Archaeology,* 16.

128. See H. Comfort in *Archaeological Discoveries in South Arabia,* 199ff.; the same for Khōr Rōrī in *BASOR* 160 (1960), 15ff.

129. See Y. Calvet in *Raydan* 5 (1988), 53ff.

CHRONOLOGY

Please note that the following dates have been assigned according to the "Long Chronology." With respect to prehistorical dates, please refer to the corresponding chapter.[1]

3rd millennium B.C.— mid-2nd millennium	Bronze Age civilizations in the area of Khaulān aṭ-Ṭiyāl
Late 3rd millennium	First irrigation facilities in Mārib
Starting 1500 B.C.	Al-Markaba settlement in the Wadi Dhana
Second half of the 2nd millennium B.C.	Heyday of the Bronze Age coastal civilization of Ṣabir
Last quarter of the 2nd millennium B.C.–1st century B.C.	Bi'r Ḥamad settlement
Starting around 1500 B.C.	Founding of settlement in Shabwa
Starting 1300 B.C.	Settlements in the Wadi al-Jūbah
10th-9th century B.C.	(Proto-)Sabaean settlement in the Wadi Yalā
10th-8th century (?)	Emergence of the South Arabian alphabet
10th century B.C.	Queen of Sheba (Saba') Visit to King Solomon
9th-8th century B.C.	Hajar bin Ḥumeid settlement
8th–mid-6th century	Saba' settles permanently in Abyssinia Start of the mukarrib period in Saba'

Mid-8th century	Governor of Suchu and Mari raided caravans from Saba’
715 B.C.	Yiṯa‘’amar of Saba’ Pays tribute to Sargon II
685 B.C.	Karibilu (Karib’īl) of Saba’ Pays tribute to Sanherib. Construction of the city wall of Mārib begins
685 (?) (400)	Karib’īl Watār Campaign against ’Ausān and destruction of that kingdom. First inscriptural mention of Qatabān
665 B.C.	Yada‘’il Dhārih built three temples for the god ’Almaqah: Maḥram Bilqis/’Awwām near Mārib, in Ṣirwāḥ, and near al-Masājid
Second half of the 6th century B.C.	Building of the Mārib Dam
Around 420	First Minaean royal inscription
Starting in 400 B.C. (350 or 300)	Kingdoms of Ma‘īn and Qatabān gain independence
Between 390 and 300	Saba’ suffers serious defeat against Qatabān
Mid-4th century B.C.	The Minaeans replace Saba’ as rulers of the incense route
4th century B.C.	Ḥaḍramaut, up to then vassal of Saba’, gains independence
4th or 3rd century B.C.	Saba’ starts minting coins.
Last quarter of the 2nd century B.C.	Wars between the various kingdoms. Ma‘īn and Qatabān are the first to disappear (according to Pirenne, 100 and 250 A.D., respectively).

115 B.C.	Beginning of the Ḥimyar era.
25-24 B.C.	Campaign by Aelius Gallus
10 A.D. (?)	
20 A.D.	Ḥimyar conquers parts of Sabaʾ and sets up its capital at Ẓafār.
Between 100 and 200 A.D.	Ḥaḍramaut annexes the rest of Qatabān.
Last quarter of the 2nd century A.D.	The traditional dynasty in Mārib is replaced by the Hamdān dynasty. Mārib's role is reduced to that of a religious center.
Last quarter of the 2nd century A.D.	Alhān Nahfān of the Hamdān dynasty becomes allied with the Abyssinians
Around 217-218	Shaʿirum Awtar, ʿAlhān Nahfān's son, fights against the Abyssinians. He also conquers the Ḥaḍramaut army and pillages Shabwa.
Around 248-49	Hamdānids forced to relinquish power to the Gurat dynasty
Starting in the second half of the 3rd century	Only two kingdoms still exist: the Sabaeo-Ḥimyar (dominated by the Ḥimyarites), and the Ḥaḍramaut kingdom.
End of the 3rd century	Shammar Yuharʿish, Ḥimyar ruler, conquers Ḥaḍramaut. Shabwa disappears from history. Shibam becomes the new capital.
Before 297	Shammar Yuharʿish sends his governor in Ṣaʿda as an ambassador to the court of the Sasanids in Seleucia-Ctesiphon.

Early 4th century	Ḥaḍramaut liberates itself from Sabaeo-Ḥimyar rule, but is then ultimately conquered in the second decade of the 4th century.
First half of the 4th century	ʿĒzānā, Abyssinian king, conquers parts of Yemen.
Mid-4th century	The Roman emperor Constantine II sends a delegation to Ẓafār; the Ḥimyar ruler converts to Christianity.
Second half of the 4th century	First break in the Mārib Dam. End of polytheism in the Sabaeo-Ḥimyar kingdom. ʾAlmaqah and other deities were replaced by Raḥmānān ("ruler of the heavens")
First third of the 5th century	Abūkarib Asʿad. Sabaeo-Ḥimyar kingdom experiences a new pinnacle.
450 A.D.	Another break in the Mārib Dam.
516	Maʿdikarib Yaʿfur leads a military campaign to Central Arabia.
517	Yūsuf Asʾar Yaṭʿar (Dhū-Nuwās) Beginning of persecution of Christians.
518 or 523	Najrān is taken and the Christians there are killed.
525	Ella Aṣbaḥā (Kālēb), Abyssinian king, defeats the Sabaeo-Ḥimyar army, and Yūsuf is killed. South Arabia comes under Abyssinian rule.
530-31	Abrehā assumes power.
542	Yet another break in the Mārib Dam.

554	Last Ḥimyar inscription.
Around 570	Abrehā leads a campaign again Mecca and dies a short time later.
6th or 7th century	Kinda dynasty in Central Arabia settles permanently in Ḥaḍramaut.
Between 570 and 575	Groups in South Arabia that are friendly toward the Persians contact the Sasanids, and the Abyssinians are forced to retreat from South Arabia.
575-580	Final break in the Mārib Dam.
597-598	South Arabia becomes a Sasanid province.
628	The Sasanids suffer a decisive defeat against Byzantium.
630	Muhammad conquers Mecca.
	Bādhān, the Sasanid governor in Yemen, converts to Islam.
632	al-Aswad alʿAnsī, a counter-prophet, leads a revolt but is defeated.
End of 630	al-Muhājir becomes the first governor of the al-Yaman province in the Muslim empire.

1. Kitchen (see esp. 175ff.) includes a very detailled time-line of the rulers in the different South Arabian kingdoms; more recently, see also "Zeittafeln" (Chronological Tables), in *Vienna Catalogue,* 418ff.

ABBREVIATIONS

AAE	*Arabian Archaeology and Epigraphy*, Copenhagen
ABADY	*Archäologische Berichte aus dem Yemen* (Archaeological Reports from Yemen), German Archaeological Institute, Sana, starting in 1982, Mainz, Germany
AfO	Archiv für Orientforschung (Archives for Middle East Research), Berlin, Germany and Graz, Austria
AION	*Annali del Istituto Orientale di Napoli*, Naples, Italy
ANRW	*Aufstieg und Niedergang der römischen Welt. Geschichte und Kultur Roms im Spiegel der neueren Forschung* (The Rise and Fall of the Roman World: History and Culture of Rome as reflected in recent research), H. Temporini and W. Hasse, eds., vol. II, 9, tome 1, Berlin and New York
L'Arabie antique	C. Robin, ed., *L'Arabie antique de Karibʾil à Mahomet,* Revue du Monde Musulman et de la Méditerranée, no. 61 (1991-1993), Aix-en-Provence, France
L'Arabie préislamique	T. Fahd, ed., *L'Arabie préislamique et son environment historique et culturel,* Actes du Colloque de Strasbourg 24-27 juin 1987 (1989), Leiden.
Arabien	A. Grohmann, *Handbuch der Altertumswissenschaft, Kulturgeschichte des Alten Orients,* sec. 3, subsec. 4, Munich 1963.
BASOR	*Bulletin of the American Schools of Oriental Research*, Jerusalem and Baghdad

Beiträge	H. von Wissmann and Maria Höfner, *Beiträge zur historischen Geographie des vorislamischen Südarabien,* Akademie der Wissenschaften und Literatur Mainz, Abhandlungen der Geistes- und Sozialw. (Mainz Academy of Sciences and Literature, Treatises in the Humanities and Social Sciences), class 1952, no. 4, Wiesbaden 1953.
BiOr	Bibliotheca Orientalis, Leiden
BSOAS	*Bulletin of the School of Oriental and African Studies*, London
CRAI	Comptes rendus de l'Académie des Inscriptions et Belles-Lettres, Paris
East and West, EW	Quarterly published by the Istituto Italiano per il Medio ed Estremo Oriente (ISMEO), Rome
EI	*Encyclopaedia of Islam*, new ed., starting 1979, Leiden and Paris
La Grèce et Saba	J. Pirenne, *La Grèce et Saba,* une nouvelle base pour la chronologie sud-arabe, Mémoires présentés par divers savants à l'Académie des Inscriptions et Belles-Lettres 15, Paris 1955.
L'Institution Monarchique	J. Ryckmans, *L'Institution Monarchique en Arabie Méridionale avant l'Islam (Maʿīn et Saba), Bibliothèque du Muséon* 28 (1951), Louvain.
Jemen Katalog	Jemen (W. Daum, ed.), *Catalogue of the Yemen exhibition in Munich*; 1987, Innsbruck, Frankfurt/Main
Jemen Report	*Mitteilungen der Deutsch-Jemenitischen Gesellschaft e.V.* (Reports of the German-Yemenite Society), Stuttgart

JEOL	*Jaarbericht van het Vooraz. Egyptisch-Genootsch.* Ex Oriente Lus, Leiden
JNES	*Journal of Near Eastern Studies*, Chicago
ÖAkWS	Österreichische Akademie der Wissenschaft (Austrian Academy of Science), phil.-hist. Kl., session reports, Vienna
Paléographie	J. Pirenne, *Paléographie des Inscriptions sud-arabes,* vol. 1: *Verhandelingen van de Koninkijke Vlaamse Academie voor Wetenschappen, Letteren en Schone Kunsten van Belgie. Klasse der Letteren,* no. 26, Brussels, 1956.
PSAS	*Proceedings of the Seminar for Arabian Studies*, London
RE	Pauly-Wissowa, *Real-Encyclopädie der classischen Altertumswissenschaft,* 1894ff, Munich
Reallexikon	*Reallexikon für Antike und Christentum*, Stuttgart 1950ff.
Studies	*Studies in the History of Arabia,* vol. 2: "Pre-Islamic Arabia." Proceedings of the 2nd International Symposium on Studies of Arabia, 13-19 April 1979, Riyadh 1984.
Syria	*Revue d'art oriental et d'archeologie,* published by the French Institute of Archeology of the Near East, Paris
Vienna Catalogue	*Jemen. Kunst und Archäologie im Land der Königin von Saba'. Ausstellungskatalog des Kunsthistorischen Museums Wien 1998/99* (Catalogue of the Jemen exhibition at the Vienna Museum of Art History), Vienna and Milan 1998.

Al-Yaman calendar	*Kalender al-Yaman,* Calendar prepared for the South Arabia exhibition, 16 November 1990-31 March 1991, Johanneum Castle Stainz, Styria, Austria

BIBLIOGRAPHY

I. Geography

1934. J. A. Montgomery, *Arabia and the Bible,* Philadelphia
1953. H. von Wissmann, "Geographie, Grundlagen und Frühzeit der Geschichte Südarabiens," in *Saeculum* 4, 61ff.
1968. H. von Wissmann, *Zur Archäologie und antiken Geographie von Südarabien, Hadramaut, Qataban und das Aden-Gebiet in der Antike,* Istanbul
1980. E. Wohlfahrt, *Die Arabische Halbinsel, Länder zwischen Rotem Meer und Persischem Golf,* Frankfurt a.M., Vienna.
1982. I. Ephe'al, *The Ancient Arabs. Nomads on the borders of the fertile crescent 9th-5th centuries B.C.,* Jerusalem.

II. People

1957. H. Pöch, "Über die äthiopide und die gondide Rasse und ihre Verbreitung," in *Anthropologischer Anzeiger* 21, 147ff., Stuttgart.
1963. A. Grohmann, *Arabien,* Munich.
1975. H. von Wissmann, *Über die frühe Geschichte Arabiens und das Entstehen des Sabäerreiches. Die Geschichte von Saba'* I, *ÖAkWS* 301, Vienna.

III. Language and Writing

1954. M. Höfner, "Das Südarabische der Inschriften und lebenden Mundarten," in *Handbuch der Orientalistik,* vol. 3: "Semitistik," 314ff., Leiden.
1956. J. Pirenne, *Paléographie,* Brussels.
1976. H. von Wissmann, "Die Geschichte des Sabäerreichs und der Feldzug des Aelius Gallus," in *ANRW* II, 9.1, 308ff.
1987. G. Garbini, "Semitische und indoeuropäische Sprachen," in *Jemen Katalog,* 107ff., Munich, Innsbruck, and Frankfurt a.M.

1987. A. F. L. Beeston, "Vorislamische Inschriften und vorislamische Sprachen des Jemen," in *Jemen Katalog,* 102ff, Munich, Innsbruck, and Frankfurt a.M.
1991-1993. C. Robin, ed., *L'Arabie antique.* This volume includes several articles on language and writing.

IV. Exploration History

1963. A. Grohmann, *Arabien,* 93ff., Munich.
1984. J. Chelhoud, ed., *L'Arabie du Sud, histoire et civilisation, le peuple yemenite et ses raines,* tome 1, 91ff., 111ff., Paris.
1985. J. Pirenne, *A la découverte de l'Arabie—cinq siècles de science et d'aventure,* Paris.

V. History

1955. J. Pirenne, *La Grèce et Saba,* Paris.
1961. J. Pirenne, *Le Royaume Sud-Arabe de Qataban et sa Datation d'après l'Archéologie et les Sources Classiques jusqu'an Périple de la Mer Erythree, Bibliothèque du Muséon* 48, Louvain.
1964. H. von Wissmann, *Zur Geschichte und Landeskunde von Alt-Südarabien, Sammlung Eduard Glaser* III, *ÖAkWS* 246, Vienna.
1976. H. von Wissmann, "Die Geschichte des Sabäerreichs und der Feldzug des Aelius Gallus," in *ANRW* II, 9.1, 308ff., Berlin and New York. This work also includes an extensive bibliography.
1976. H. von Wissmann, *Über die frühe Geschichte Arabiens und das Entstehen des Sabäerreiches. Die Geschichte von Saba'* I, *ÖAkWS* 301, Vienna.
1982. H. von Wissmann, *Die Geschichte von Saba'* II: Das Grossreich der Sabäer bis zu seinem Ende im frühen 4. Jh. vor Chr., *ÖAkWS* 402, Vienna.
1984. W. W. Müller, "Survey of the Arabian Peninsula from the first century A.D. to the rise of Islam," in *Studies,* 125ff.
1987. W. W. Müller, "Skizze der Geschichte Altsüdarabiens," *Jemen Katalog,* 56ff., Munich, Innsbruck, and Frankfurt a.M.
1989. Toufin Fahd, ed., *L'Arabie préislamique,* Leiden.

1990. M. ʿAbd al-Qadir Bafiqih, *L'Unification du Yemen antique. La lutte entre Saba, Himyar et la Ladramaut du Ier au IIIeme siècles de l'ère chrétienne,* Bibliothèque de Raydan, Paris.

1991-1993. C. Robin, ed., *L'Arabie antique,* Aix-en-Provence (with an extensive bibliography).

1994. K. A. Kitchen, *The World of Ancient Arabia Series. Documents for Ancient Arabia,* part I: Chronological Framework and Historical Sources, Liverpool.

VI. Archaeology

1994. G. Caton-Thompson, *The Tombs and Moon Temple of Hureidha (Hadhramaut),* Reports Research Comm., Soc. of Antiquaries of London, no. 13, London.

1958. R. LeBaron Bowen, Jr. and F. P. Albright, *Archaeological Discoveries in South Arabia.* With contributions by B. Segall, J. Ternbach, A. Jamme, H. Comford, G. W. Van Beek, Publ. of the Am. Foundation for the Study of Man, vol. II, Baltimore.

1964. G. Lankester Harding, *Archaeology in the Aden Protectorates,* London.

1969. G. W. Van Beek, *Hajar bin Humeid. Investigations at a Pre-Islamic Site in South Arabia.* Publ. of the Am. Foundation for the Study of Man, vol. V, Baltimore.

1971. B. Doe, *Southern Arabia,* London.

1982. *Archäologische Berichte aus dem Yemen,* Deutsches Arch. Institute Sanʿa, vol. I (ed. J. Schmidt), Mainz. A total of eight volumes were published up to 1995.

1982. F. P. Albright, *The American Archaeological Expedition in Dhofar, Oman 1952-1953,* Publ. of the Am. Foundation for the Study of Man, vol. VI, Washington, D.C.

1983. Brian Doe, *Monuments of South Arabia,* Naples, Cambridge, and New York.

1984. M. R. Toplyn, *The Wadi al-Jubah Project,* vol. 1: Site Reconnaissance in North-Yemen, 1982, Publ. of the Am. Foundation for the Study of Man, Washington, D.C.

1985. J. A. Blakely, J. A. Sauer, and M. R. Toplyn, *The Stratigraphic*

Probe at Hajar at-Tamrah. The Wadi al-Jubah Project, vol. 2, Publ. of the Am. Foundation for the Study of Man, Washington, D.C.

1987. W. Glanzman and Abdu O. Ghaleb, *The Stratigraphic Probe at Hajar ar-Rayhani, The Wadi al-Jubah Project,* vol. 3, Publ. of the Am. Foundation for the Study of Man, Washington, D.C.

1988. A. de Maigret, ed., *The Sabaean Archaeological Complex in the Wadi Yala. A Preliminary Report.* Reports and Memoirs (ISMEO) 21, Rome.

1990. A. de Maigret, ed., *The Bronze Age culture of Hawlan at Tiyal and al-Hada.* Reports and Memoirs (ISMEO) 24, Rome.

1991. J.-F. Breton, "Les Fouilles de Shabwa," in *Syria* 68, Paris. This report is identical to *Fouilles de Shabwa* II, which appeared in 1992.

VI. Social Structures

1951. J. Ryckmans, *L'Institution Monarchique,* Louvain.

1971. A. F. L. Beeston, "Functional Significance of the Old South Arabian Town," *PSAS* 1, 26ff., London.

1982. C. Robin, *Les Hautes-Terres du Nord-Yemen avant Islam,* vols. I, II, Publ. de l'Institut historique-archéologique neerlandais de Stambuul, Instanbul.

1984. C. Robin, "La Cité et l'Organisation Sociale à Maᶜin: L'Exemple de YIL (Aujourd'hui Baraqish)," in *Studies,* 157ff.

VII. Economy

1922. A. Grohmann, *Südarabien als Wirtschaftsgebiet,* part I: "Osten und Orient," *Erste Reihe Forschungen* 4, Vienna.

1933. A. Grohmann, *Südarabien als Wirtschaftsgebiet,* part II, Brünn.

1978. W. W. Müller, "Weihrauch," in *RE,* suppl. vol. 15 (1978), col. 700ff., Munich.

1981. H. Kopp, *Agrargeographie der Arabischen Republik Jemen. Landnutzung und agrarsoziale Verhältnisse in einem islamisch-orientalischen Entwicklungsland mit alter bäuerlicher Kultur,*

Erlanger Geographische Arbeiten, spec. vol. 11, Erlangen.
1989. M. Höfner, "Landwirtschaft im antiken Südarabien," in *Grazer Morgenländische Studien 2: Der orientalische Mensch und seine Beziehungen zur Umwelt.* Beiträge zum 2. Grazer Morgenländischen Symposion (2-5 March 1989), ed. B. Scholz, Graz.
1991. I. Hehmeyer and J. Schmidt, *Antike Technologie—Die sabäische Wasserwirtschaft von Marib, ABADY* 1, Mainz.

VIII. Military

1976. A. F. L. Beeston, *Warfare in Ancient South Arabia (2nd-3rd centuries A.D.),* Qahtan, Studies in Old South Arabian Epigraphy, Fasc. 3, London.
1994. J.-F. Breton, *Les Fortifications d'Arabie Méridionale du 7e au 1er siècle avant notre Ere, ABADY* 7, Mainz.

IX. Religion(s)

1927. D. Nielsen, "Zur altarabischen Religion," in *Handbuch der altarabischen Altertumskunde,* ed. D. Nielsen, vol. 1: "Die altarabische Kultur," 177ff., Copenhagen.
1951. G. Ryckmans, *Les religions arabes préislamique,* 2nd ed., *Bibliothèque de Muséon* 26, Louvain.
1956. A. Jamme, "La religion arabe préislamique," in M. Brillant and R. Aigrain, eds., *Histoire des Religions* 4, Tournai.
1970. M. Höfner, "Die Religionen Altsyriens, Altarabiens und der Mandäer," in *Religionen der Menschheit* 10, no. 2, 234ff., Stuttgart.
1987. J. Ryckmans, "Die Altsüdarabische Religion," in *Jemen Katalog,* 111ff., Innsbruck, Frankfurt a.M.
1992. J. Ryckmans, "Religion of South Arabia," in *The Anchor Bible Dictionary,* ed. D. N. Freedman, vol. 6, 171ff., New York.

X. Art

1955. J. Pirenne, *La Grèce et Saba,* Paris.

1963. A. Grohmann, *Arabien,* 140-243, Munich.
1979. A. Hauptmannn–von Gladiss, "Probleme altsüdarabischer Plastik," in *Baghdader Mitteilungen* 10, 145ff., Berlin.
1982. Starting in 1982, *Archäologische Berichte aus dem Yemen* (ABADY) has been offering information in the area of art, especially architecture.
1987. The *Jemen Katalog* also has articles dealing with art.
1988. M. Jung, "The Religious Monuments of Ancient South Arabia," in *AION* 48, 177ff., Naples.
1993. J.-F. Breton and M. ʿAbd al-Qādir Bāfaqīh, eds., *Trésors du Wādī Dura (République du Yemen. Fouille franco-yéménite de la nécropole de Hajar am-Dhaybiyya).* Institut Français d'Archéologie du Proche-Orient. *Bibliothéque Archéologique et Historique* 141, Paris.

INDEX OF PERSONS

INDEX OF PLACE NAMES

SUBJECT INDEX

KLAUS SCHIPPMAN, professor of archaeology at the university of Göttingen, Germany, is the author of numerous books, including:

Die iranischen Feuerheiligtümmer
Grundzüge der parthischen Geschichte
Les reliefs rupestres d'Elymaide (Iran) de l'epoche parthe (with L. Vanden Berghe)
Grundzüge der Geschichte des sasanidischen Reiches.

ALLISON BROWN has translated numerous books and articles from German to English, including:

Gisela Bock, *Women in European History*
Gad Beck, *An Underground Life: The Memoirs of a Gay Jew in Nazi Berlin*
Dan Diner, *America in the Eyes of the Germans: An Essay on Anti-Americanism*
Horst Bredekamp, *The Lure of Antiquity and the Cult of the Machine: The Kunstkammer and the Evolution of Nature, Art and Technology*
Heinz Halm, *Sh'ia Islam: From Religion to Revolution*